FEB 0 5 2004	**DATE DUE**		

D1022797

Mitch Murray's
HANDBOOK
FOR THE
TERRIFIED
SPEAKER

VALIUM IN A VOLUME

---

foulsham
LONDON • NEW YORK • TORONTO • SYDNEY

foulsham

The Publishing House, Bennetts Close,
Cippenham, Slough, Berkshire, SL1 5AP, England

Edited by Carole Chapman

ISBN 0-572-02459-2

Copyright © 1999 Mitch Murray

Other books by the same author include:
Mitch Murray's One-Liners For Weddings
Mitch Murray's One-Liners For Business and
Mitch Murray's One-Liners For Speeches On Special Occasions.

Printed in Great Britain by St. Edmundsbury Press, Bury St. Edmunds, Suffolk

Contents

DEDICATION

In recent years, the word 'partner' has come to mean someone you're sleeping with. Back in the late sixties and seventies, I had a partner I really rated but wouldn't *dream* of sleeping with: Peter Callander, my collaborator, co-writer and co-owner of several music publishing and record production interests. He was the greatest partner anyone could wish for. Peter was – and is – wise, pragmatic, fair-minded and totally honest. It's just a shame we have nothing in common.

He's still one of my closest friends and I'm proud to dedicate this book to him and his family.

You did say £50, didn't you Peter?

Names and characters in this book are used solely for the purpose of example. Any similarity between these fictional illustrations and real people is entirely coincidental.

So put that lawyer away and don't be silly!

Sting and 'Thing'

Foreword

When Mitch Murray invited me to write the foreword to his new book, I was intrigued and flattered. After all, I have based my entire songwriting career on the words of wisdom in his first masterpiece *How To Write A Hit Song*, which I read in 1965 when I was fourteen.

As I remember, it featured pics of him carrying Hammond organs into the Flamingo Club and loitering artfully against Victorian lampposts in Denmark Street, and musing over a blank sheet of manuscript while chewing the end of a Bic ballpoint pen.

Yes my friends, I owe it all to Mitch.

I have managed to carve a career out of a small and arguably dubious talent for matching melodies and rhyming couplets and, of course, have been more than amply rewarded for a pastime that I would have gladly indulged in whether I got paid or not, and there are far more unpleasant ways of making a living.

When I first read the synopsis of this new book I wondered if, having made a songwriter of me, Mitch Murray could now miraculously turn me into an after-dinner speaker. It's quite a challenge.

I know from bitter experience that singers, like footballers, should never speak. The magic and illusion that music, and skill with a football can create, is instantly and cruelly dispelled as soon as one of us opens our mouths.

About ten years ago I started mouthing off about the destruction of the rainforests. Well, more trees have been burned in the last ten years than in any time in the world's history – not my fault entirely but you see my point.

'Shut up and sing, you pillock' was the considered response of the vox populi and, of course, they are always right.

I will still warble on at length on the subject when prompted, but no one seems to take a blind bit of notice. Although I will have to restrain myself from saying 'I told you so!' when bits the size of Europe start detaching themselves from the Arctic ice fields and we start suffering from heat-stroke in the middle of an English winter.

All right, I'll stop ...

But, if any book can make *me* funny, Paul Gascoigne urbane or Kenny Dalglish and the Gallagher brothers the epitome of charm and sparkling wit, then it certainly deserves some sort of prize.

And, take it from me, if anyone can turn you into an after-dinner speaker, Mitch Murray can.

Introduction

The fear of speaking in public has always been a powerful challenge.
It is often a frightening reality which can haunt a speech-maker from the very moment he or she receives the assignment.

Until now, no book, no therapist, no drug has ever been able to do very much to relieve this dreadful anxiety.

Obviously they've been missing the point.

If you were to ask your average terrified speaker to articulate his fear, he couldn't.

There's a very good reason for this.

It's not one fear. It's a whole *bunch* of fears.

◆ It's the fear of not being able to think up and put together a fast-moving witty, well-constructed speech of relevance and substance.

◆ It's the fear of offending some members of the audience, whilst managing to bore the pants off the rest.

◆ It's the fear of not *looking* right: awkward posture, trembling hands, fumbling with notes.

◆ It's the fear of not *sounding* right: stammering, speaking too quickly, not being heard.

God, this is pathetic!

◆ It's the fear of forgetting lines, topics, important facts.

◆ It's the fear of going on too long.

◆ It's the fear of not saying enough.

◆ It's the fear of a hostile crowd.

◆ It's the fear of a bored crowd.

◆ It's the fear of ridicule.

Hey, this is getting *me* frightened now. I'd better stop.

This book is the first piece of work designed to address these individual concerns and break them down into manageable segments.

It won't eradicate every fear. It couldn't, and as it happens it shouldn't. Some fears are *good* fears.

Don't forget, it was fear that drove you to buy this book in the first place. Now *there's* a good fear.
Well, good for me anyway.

Even the most experienced professionals admit to a few palpitations before making a speech. Nerves can make a positive contribution. You *need* one or two pretty little butterflies. These can be useful creatures, pollinating just enough adrenaline to give your performance that extra bit of magic. This heightened state of excitement provides you with a certain edge and helps you achieve concentration and clarity of thought; your performance will be all the better for it.

A little healthy apprehension can be useful even at an earlier stage. Your research will be more thorough and you'll be alert to the possible pitfalls surrounding your performance on the night. A spoonful of 'good fear' will drive you to make sure that details such as lighting, sound and your speaking position in the room are as favourable as possible.

Of course, I don't expect all this 'good fear' stuff to be in the least reassuring for you at this point. After all, you've probably only just been lumbered with that forthcoming speaking engagement. As long as you don't think about it, you're fine. Then, suddenly, something reminds you of your impending ordeal. All at once, your heartbeat quickens, you have trouble swallowing, you feel hot and cold and there's a bloody great scorpion crawling around in your stomach. You can't identify exactly which bits of the approaching speechmaking process are causing you to panic. All you know is that this looming prospect is threatening to spoil your life!

Well, my trembling friend, salvation is at hand. Uncle Mitch has arrived and all will be well. Each of your fears is about to be isolated, diagnosed and treated.

These are the targets in your war of worries and, like a row of sitting ducks on a fairground stall, it's time to start picking them off one by one.

So load your gun, breathe in and prepare to take your first shot. And if at first you miss, well, I suppose it's better to be scared stiff than not stiff at all.

Wow! What a writer *this* guy turned out to be!

Make it Easy on Yourself

Let's start by establishing an overall strategy; we're going to avoid making a big deal out of this speech thing. Agreed?

If there's a short cut, we'll take it.

If there's a dirty trick, we'll pull it.

If there's a wild card, we'll play it.

The whole idea is to relieve as much pressure on you as possible without compromising the quality of your finished result.

I don't care how nervous you are – that's purely a matter between you and your laundry – but let's not make it worse. Let's take the fast track. Let's go the easy route.

Some people rise at six every morning, put in thirteen or fourteen hours of really hard work and think nothing of it.

I'm like that myself. I don't think much of it either.

My motto has always been: 'Don't Work Hard, Work Well!' Very often, the easier route is also the best. Now isn't *that* good news?

This book is full of crafty little devices designed to make

the whole thing as trouble free as possible. Make full use of them. If you can apply an instinctive approach to the entire process, the result will sound and look natural, smooth and cool.

A good speech should appear almost effortless. Nothing makes an audience more nervous than an over-written, over-performed, contrived address – and if your audience is nervous, what chance have *you* got? So make it easy on yourself and make it easy on them.

Want some more good news?

You don't have to learn that speech by heart. In fact, you won't need to memorise anything. With a few simple techniques, I'll show you how to keep your audience blissfully unaware that you're reading every word.

Furthermore, once you read about my fiendishly clever Colourtext system, you'll never have to worry about losing your place in the script.

That's right: make it easy on yourself.

It's useful to know that audiences have their own reward system. They award points in the form of laughter and bonus points in the form of applause.

- You get points when you surprise them, amuse them and delight them.

- You get *bonus* points for topicality, for ingenuity and for sitting down.

- You get *no* points for length.

So make it easy on yourself – keep it short.

Speechmaking – whether social, political or corporate – can only ever be an exercise in superficiality.
It simply isn't a medium which allows you unlimited expansion and embellishment of your thoughts.
Give a speech too much substance and it becomes a lecture.

People, nowadays, are programmed to absorb soundbites.
After years of media conditioning, the attention span of an average audience now roughly equates to that of a stick of broccoli.

It gets worse!

The more intelligent the crowd, the less patience they have.

No matter how important the subject, you have to resist the temptation to expand every argument, examine every area and explore every avenue.
If, for example, you're giving a business presentation, don't go in for the kind of detail the Prosecution pursued in the OJ Simpson trial or *your* Jury will kick you up the bum as well.
Far better to make a punchy, interesting speech and supply them with a set of supporting documentation which they can take away with them and probably bin later.

Hey, at least you tried.

A modern speech needs bullet points, catchy words and humour. These spoken headlines have to be linked together with little verbal bridges and will need to follow a logical path.
Don't allow yourself to be haunted by the fear that your speech only scratches the surface of the subject. In most cases, that's all they want. Your modest aim should be to raise and illustrate topics in an informative and entertaining way.

Those of you who are familiar with my other books will know that I am a keen proponent of speeches which make use of one-liners rather than anecdotes and longer stories. This type of speech is even more desirable if you happen to be a nervous speaker craving acceptance. It's most reassuring to get regular reactions from the audience throughout your piece.

I'm not suggesting that every type of speech needs to be packed with gags and zingers. If the speech has a serious purpose or a sombre setting, you could be in danger of coming across as flippant and shallow if you overdo it. The trick is to know how often to punctuate your performance with humour, and to choose the appropriate style.

> The *positioning* of certain material makes an important difference. A controversial one-liner or comment which could sound crass and vulgar at the beginning of your piece, may be happily accepted and appreciated once your audience has been warmed up and nurtured into a state of readiness. There's no great trick to this nurturing stuff; just hold back the riskier lines until the crowd trusts your good taste and judgement, then prove 'em wrong big time.

Even the best speeches are studded with a combination of little successes, droplets of indifference and occasional failures.
By using one-liners, you are in a position to disguise the failures, weather the indifference and milk the successes.

Ultimately, what's the worst that could happen? Even if you die a death, it's not as if you've been addressing the Security Council in order to save your country from invasion.
Since when did a speech to *that* lot do any good anyway?

Just do what you do. You don't have to write another 'I have a dream!'. For one thing, look what happens to the guys who make earth-shattering speeches like that:

Martin Luther King: 'I have a dream ... ' – Bang!

John F. Kennedy: 'Ask not what your country can do for you ... ' – Bang!

Abe Lincoln: 'Fourscore and seven years ago ... ' – Bang!

Irving Berlin: 'I'm Dreaming Of A White Christmas ... '
– Bing!

So try to bear my laid-back strategy in mind. Don't make a tough assignment tougher. Don't allow your fears to become self-fulfilling. Be thorough, be strong, but don't try too hard.

Do like the Walker Brothers said: Make it easy on yourself.

Think it Through

I'm sure you've heard that old cliché about a survey which purported to show that people are less frightened of *dying* than making a speech.

What a load of old tosh!

Believe me, if some psycho pointed a loaded .38 at your temple and said, 'Make a speech or die!', your instant response would be, 'My lords, ladies and gentlemen ... '

There's no doubt about it. You can certainly do it if you have to.

But do you *have* to? Couldn't you just say 'No'?

Is it your vanity which trapped you into agreeing to this ordeal, or are you doing it because no other bugger would?

Stop and think: can you get out of it? And *should* you?

If you answered 'yes' to both of these questions, bye bye and thanks for reading this far. (Sorry, no refunds.)

If you're still with me, I assume it's because you have no choice. For one reason or another, this is a speech you simply *have* to make.

Okay. Let's get cracking.

Start by clearing all the clutter from your mind. Step back away from those trees and take a broad overview of the forest.

Take time out to think everything through, it could save you a lot of grief.

THINK ABOUT THE SETTING

Is it social? Is it business? Or is it something in between? Your tone and the language you use will largely depend on these distinctions.

A speaker, who may be quite comfortable making business presentations, could suddenly find himself called upon to give his daughter away at her wedding. Straight away, there's a problem.

This poor guy is out of his depth, and he knows it.

Whereas he's quite used to praising a product or talking about a service, this is quite different. He's now expected to express his feelings, to expose his sentiments. It's become *personal*.

Suddenly our businessman somehow has to be transformed into an emotional flasher.

He needs to show his daughter the love and affection he really feels for her, yet he can't be too gushing. It's not his style.

Later in the book, you'll be reading about the 'Ping Pong' method – my special technique for faking sincerity whilst avoiding going over the top and nauseating your audience. 'Ping Pong' can be equally effective in a business setting, a charity speech or any other situation where it's .important to stay on-message without being too intense.

If your only previous experience of public speaking was the time you were best man at Brian Perkin's wedding and you've just been asked to present your department's five-year marketing perspective to the board of directors, you have a similar problem but in reverse.

This time you're not Jack-the-Lad taking the piss out of a hapless bridegroom in front of a load of drunken guests, you're a young executive who needs to retain the confidence and support of some very crusty, impassive old codgers.

What you say, and the way you say it, is very important to your division and crucial to your own career.

So before you put pen to paper, think it through.

THINK ABOUT WHY YOU WERE CHOSEN

Why do they want you to make the speech?

Is it because of *what* you are or *who* you are?

Level with yourself. If you happen to be this year's President of the Merryview Golf Club, there's no debate. You're landed with the task of speaking because of *who* you are, and they're stuck with you, like it or not.

Under these circumstances, you could rise to your feet, welcome everybody, tell 'em to enjoy themselves and promptly sit down again, all within two minutes.

The audience would be so relieved, you'd probably earn yourself a standing ovation.

If, however, you have a reputation as an outrageous and witty raconteur, and the local Rotary Club has asked you to be their guest speaker, you've been invited because of *what* you are.

This is both good news and bad news.

First, the bad news. Your hosts have expectations. You have to deliver. It's no good standing up, uttering a couple of platitudes, raising your glass, then lowering your arse.
The good news is that they really don't care too much about what you say, as long as it's funny.

So take a little time to assess why they want you and just what they want *from* you. Are you speaking to entertain, to show love and respect, to inform, to motivate, to build bridges, to mend fences, or just to stop them asking you again?

Think it through.

THINK ABOUT THE TOPIC

In most cases, the subject of a speech is a foregone conclusion: someone's birthday, a retirement, a chairman's report.
As a speechmaker, you have to avoid sounding like you merely pulled something off the shelf and changed around a few names or issues.
If it's a social speech, it should sound natural to the ear, personal to the individuals involved and suitable for the atmosphere of the occasion.
If it's a business speech, it should come across as authoritative yet measured, well-informed yet relaxed, and appropriate to the corporate identity.

The crucial element in all this, is research.

Your starting point when preparing any speech with a pre-determined subject, is to collect lots and lots of information.
If the focal point of your talk is a person, you'll need biographical notes and a reasonable knowledge of their

special characteristics, positive qualities and foibles.

If you're speaking to an organisation, you'll be investigating its history, aims, corporate policy and any current issues facing the company or the association concerned.

If your information is sketchy and you come up against a brick wall, do the best you can. Research just enough to chuck a credible line in here and there, and link to what *you* would like to talk about.

The technique to get you seamlessly out of one topic and into another is the clever use of 'bridging lines' and 'link words'.

I bet you can't wait to hear about those little devils, can you?

There are many ways to gather and arrange material for speeches on specific subjects, and you'll be reading about them quite soon.

Every now and then, however, a speaker is given carte-blanche as to the choice of topic, and this often proves to be a most difficult challenge.

After all, where do you start?

I once had the pleasure of travelling across the Atlantic aboard the *QE2*. As a first-class passenger (what other kind is there?) I was able to dine in the ship's top restaurant, The Queen's Grill.

When I asked the waiter what my choices were, he said, 'We'll be happy to make you absolutely anything; what would you like?'

If I'd been presented with four or five options for each course, I'd have had no problem choosing my meal. Faced with Epicurean infinity, however, I agonised for ages before placing my order. I had no starting point, no inspiration, no basis for a positive way forward.

The same dilemma applies when, as a speaker, you've been allowed total freedom to choose the theme of your speech. Believe me, your hosts are doing you no favours, although, undeniably, their confidence in your abilities is flattering.

In this situation, you'd be well advised to look back at the previous section and ask yourself why you were chosen. Are you the life and soul of the party? Are you an expert at something? Have you had an interesting life?

The answer may provide you with a subject, or at least point you in the right direction. But here's a warning: unless you happen to be a super-celebrity, don't talk too much about *you*. The people in the audience really prefer to hear about themselves.

When I make an after-dinner speech, I avoid going on too long about myself, even though I'm one *hell* of a guy.
Having thoroughly researched the organisation concerned and the characters within it, I open by establishing my credentials with a few lines about my career. This becomes the 'hub' of the speech. I then work in a bit of business which justifies my right to send up some of the prominent people present, and begin to lay in to them. Every now and then, I link back to my story or to lines about showbusiness in general, returning to insult my hosts at regular intervals. (Don't worry, they love it.)

Some speeches are associated with a tradition, for instance 'Burns Night'.
Happily, once you have paid due deference to 'Rabbie', you can do more or less what you like. The trick is somehow to link all the Burns crap to the good stuff. You see, you're part of a conspiracy with the audience who are feigning

interest in Robert Burns in order to enjoy an entertaining evening.

'Ladies Night' is another example. As long as you start and end with some stuff about ladies, you can get away with murder.

If you've ever heard a speech made by a celebrity guest at a charity function, you may have noticed that in a fifteen minute spot, a maximum of forty seconds or so would normally be devoted to the subject itself. This is because nobody actually goes to a charity appeal to hear an appeal for charity. They go for other reasons: a pleasant get-together with friends, an excuse to wear that new sequinned evening dress (with the wife's permission, of course), an opportunity to see a well-known personality in the flesh, a chance to enjoy good food and fine wines. (That'll be the day!)
The last thing they want, is to hear someone pimping for whales, trees, seals or owls.

You may also have noticed that many celebrities are not particularly *good* at after-dinner speeches, despite the high fees they command.
Organisations will often pay big money to 'capture' a well-known name for their event, regardless of how well he or she performs on the podium. Faced with the choice of a brilliant but unknown speaker and a star from a hit TV series, what else could they do? After all, they have to sell tickets or there'll be no din-dins for anybody.

The subject of a speech may be of little consequence when an audience is ogling a big-name guest, but in your case, it matters.
So think it through.

THINK ABOUT YOUR AUDIENCE

If you're trying to put across a thoughtful analysis of your corporate strategy in front of twenty-six regional managers, the pace of your presentation will be quite different from a rousing end-of-conference 'go get 'em' blockbuster.

Should you be toasting the health of an eighty-year-old lady in front of half-a-dozen of her friends, your manner won't be anything like the delivery style you'd assume at a political rally at the Brighton Conference Centre. The type of audience, the size of the audience and the likely mood of the audience are all factors you'll need to bear in mind when writing your piece, but remember you have to sound as normal and as 'unspeechy' as you can, even if you're addressing a thousand people.

When making a speech, you have a very special relationship with the people in front of you. Everyone in the room has become part of a collective entity. You are not talking to individuals anymore, you are addressing a fusion of thought and response.

Bloody scary, isn't it? Just like *Village Of The Damned*.

As you begin to write, put yourself in the front row of the audience and imagine watching yourself make the speech. Does the content and style sound right coming from *you*? You may simply be too *young* to get away with certain lines or routines. An audience may find it hard to accept a twenty-five year-old sending up a well-respected senior, or attempting to make caustic comments on a subject or circumstance they're unlikely yet to have experienced.

A mature speaker has it much easier. He or she has lived, and everyone can see it. The greying hair, the lined face, the reading-glasses, all combine to give the older speaker an assumed authority. They are allowed to be cranky, ultra-dry and disparaging. You, on the other hand – a mere kid – could so easily come across to the audience as an upstart. Of course, a wrinkly will look ridiculous if he tries too hard to sound 'with it', when he's obviously nowhere *near* it. The audience won't buy *that* either.

Horses for courses, my son. Think it through.

THINK ABOUT THE TIME OF DAY, TRICKY SITUATIONS AND OTHER STUFF

Now I'll bet you never even *thought* about thinking about the time of day. You should you know because the clock often affects how your speech needs to be put across.

You wouldn't expect to adopt the same approach at an early morning seminar as you would for that farewell speech to a retiring colleague in the pub after hours. The composition of the crowd, the location, the nature of your message, the hour, even the season, your demeanour and delivery will have to adapt to these differing conditions.

There's always a danger when handling certain sensitive issues such as serious illness or recent bereavement, that your audience will become sombre and that your speech will end on a sad and awkward note.

If a prominent member of your cricket club happened to pass away two weeks earlier, you would naturally be expected to make some reference to the sad loss. To ignore it would look rather callous and cowardly.

The wording you adopt to deal with the situation is, of course, all important. However, you will also need to know where to place the segment in your script, how to lead into it, and how to move out of it.

The announcement of bad news needs careful consideration too. Here, humour can be very useful; a wry comment often helps keep things in proportion – but do remember, every member of that audience will be thinking, 'How does this affect me?'.
Don't be too flippant, they're pissed off enough as it is.

As you will see later in the book, there are effective ways of dealing with these issues, so hold on to my hand, be good and don't wander away.

Once you start getting deeply involved in researching, preparing and writing your speech, you could lose sight of how things will actually be when you come to perform it. It's all too easy to get lost in your own creativity. You'll be a lot more confident and relaxed about your performance on the night if you're satisfied that you've taken all these little things into account.
Re-reading these pages may prove useful as an occasional course-correction, so be prepared to return to this chapter from time to time in order to make sure you're still on track.

Keep your wits about you. Think it through.

How the Big Boys Cope

You may find it reassuring to learn that however experienced and successful a speaker or entertainer may get to be, there is no guarantee that he or she will ever be free of those dreaded butterflies. So if you suffer from the jitters, be assured you're not the only one. In fact, you're in very good company.

Frank Sinatra freely admitted that he was terrified before every single performance. For the first four or five seconds, he'd literally tremble.

David Niven used to throw up in the dressing room as he waited for his call.

Le Pétomane ... oh, never mind about Le Pétomane.

Having told you that, I'm not sure if I've made you feel better or worse. You may think it strange that people suffering from such severe and chronic stagefright, would choose to make their living in this way.
On the face of it, it makes as much sense as someone with a fear of heights deciding to become a steeplejack.
Well, here's something even stranger: some people actually *enjoy* the sensation of tension leading up to a performance.

Top comedy writer and speaker Barry Cryer doesn't like the term 'nerves', he prefers 'creative apprehension'.
'I quite like that feeling', he told me, ' ... you know, sitting

there, waiting to speak ... come on, come on, I'm ready, let's get on with it!'

'Creative apprehension' eh? What an excellent description of the effect I wrote about in the introduction.
A quick shot of self-induced adrenaline, adds a little buzz to your presentation and a touch of magic to your delivery. Without that heightened clarity of consciousness, you're liable either to make mistakes, or to give a very drab performance.
If you want an example of a calm, measured speaker, cast your mind back to Sir Geoffrey Howe – a guy who could walk into an empty room and blend right in.
No trace of adrenaline there; for him, valium would have been a *stimulant*!

As a speaker, I've always found it useful and comforting to talk and drink with my audience before I do my stuff. It helps me feel I have a few friends out there, and teaches me a little more about the people I'll be addressing.

Barry Cryer also finds it helpful to mingle with the crowd beforehand. 'I'm terminally gregarious', he admitted, 'I want to be in there among 'em.'

On occasion, Barry has been asked not to appear in the room until actually introduced. 'You're a surprise', his host would explain.
'I don't want to be a surprise', said Barry, 'it's not my thing.'
By contrast, his great friend, the late William Rushton, was quite happy to watch TV in his hotel suite until called. 'He wasn't the mingling type' Barry confided.

When we talked about pre-speech drinking, Barry said, 'After-dinner speaking is one job where it's very easy to be totally knackered before you even stand up. You have to pace yourself. Make sure your drinking is slower than all the others; just a glass or two of white wine or lager. Afterwards, of course, you can let rip.'

Jimmy Tarbuck is less compromising: 'No booze at all before the gig!'
His other rules are equally strict but simple:

◆ Choose material appropriate for the event
◆ Know what you're doing and don't do too long
◆ Make sure they can hear you

Jimmy and I once had a discussion about the difference between stand-up comedy and after-dinner speaking.
I had just made a speech during which Jimmy – a great supporter – was loudly leading the laughter.
'You should do stand-up' he said.
'I've only just sat down', I said.
'No, seriously. You ought to do it – you're hilarious.'
'Jimmy, I couldn't possibly do what you do. It's totally different. I'd be terrible at it.'

You see, when a comic goes on stage, he's confronting the audience. He's asking for laughs. If he doesn't get them, he has no place to go. An after-dinner speaker, on the other hand, is inspiring laughter as a by-product of what he's doing. Like an actor, the speaker is hiding behind a role. His justification for performing is the toast, the tribute, the vote of thanks. Unlike the comedian, his humour is not head-on – it's sneaked in.

Former rally driver, Ford executive, and Benedictine After-Dinner Speaker of the Year 1988 – Stuart Turner – is regarded as one of the funniest speechmakers in the business.
His recommended defence against pre-speech nerves is *preparation*.
In particular, Stuart stresses the importance of audience analysis but, he says, 'Beware of the organiser who tells

you they're a sober bunch – they'll be the ones singing rugby songs by coffee time.'

He favours a little 'routine', 'I like to mention to my host before speaking, one particular incident I once experienced. I *know* it's a daft thing to do and I *know* it's superstitious, but it helps. I'm a lot less nervous before lecturing a team-building session than before a purely after-dinner speech, because I'm not seeking the same reaction. As Eric Morecambe once said, "It's all based on fear!"'

Former Trappist Monk and celebrated after-dinner speaker Peter Moloney reminds us that, 'Professionalism is based on not letting the terror show, because no one can forgive you for making them feel sorry for you.'

Later in the book, under the sub-heading, 'Whistle A Happy Tune', you'll be learning how to disguise that terror.

I think it's reasonable to assume that an explorer who once undertook a six thousand mile, six month journey across the Pacific on a bamboo raft, is liable to know a thing or two about not losing one's cool.

When Rex Warner isn't exploring the Arctic, or trekking around the West Coast of Greenland, or sailing a seventy-five foot Chinese Junk in the South China Sea, he's very much in demand as an entertaining speaker. Advice from someone as fearless as Rex is certainly worth taking on board. Here it is:

◆ Only speak on subjects which you have a passion for

◆ Just before taking to the stage, try to yawn or breathe deeply

◆ Before starting to speak, breathe deeply once more, pause and smile

◆ In the first few sentences of the speech aim to relax, intrigue or challenge the audience with either humour, comments or questions

◆ Involve the audience

◆ End on a high

Rex doesn't believe in using lecterns; he sees them as a barrier between you and the audience. He says, 'What are you afraid of? Walk around, get close to the audience. If you're worried about forgetting your speech, carry your notes round with you.'

Graham Davies is a barrister at the Criminal Bar, and a sparkling corporate after-dinner speaker. He echoes my earlier statement on how difficult it is to articulate exactly what frightens us about making a speech:

'Most fear in public speaking is a vague fear of the unknown: a fear that *something* dreadful will happen during the speech.
But when you try to pin down *what* it is you are scared of, it is almost impossible.'

He continues, 'The key to conquering nerves is to change your vague, negative thoughts into specific positive thoughts. In the long term, keep thinking about all the preparation work you have done to create a brilliant script. Allow yourself to be proud of it.'

Graham suggests the use of a technique that works for professional sprinters:

'In the minutes before you speak, focus on the first step. Keep repeating your opening line in your mind. If you are focusing all your thoughts on this, your mind does not have the energy to be nervous as well.'

Solid-gold advice there from one of the best.

'The Man In The White Suit', former BBC war correspondent Martin Bell M.P. confesses, 'I have been under fire in Vietnam, dodged bullets in the Golan Heights, been shot at and injured in Bosnia, but I've never been as terrified as when I had to make a speech at my daughter's wedding.'

Martin Bell has witnessed many horrors and faced countless ordeals as a reporter. He's been ambushed, not only in Biafra and the former Yugoslavia, but also – famously – in his own constituency of Knutsford, by the formidable Christine Hamilton and her hapless husband Neil.
He's been ruthlessly cross-examined by former colleagues at press conferences and endured the nerve-racking experience of a maiden speech in the House of Commons.

Why then should the prospect of saying a few words to family and friends prove to be such a nightmare?

As a speechwriter I have come across many high-flying executives who think nothing of addressing international conferences or making presentations to hostile audiences, yet begin to quake when faced with a ten-minute wedding speech.

I highlighted this problem in my previous chapter, 'Think It Through'.

Persuasion, logic, rationalisation – all that stuff is useless now. Suddenly, the words have to come from your heart, not from your head.
It's a brand new language: one of emotion, affection, gratitude, love.

There's the difference.

In Martin Bell's case, there was an added dimension. He told me, 'There are no retakes in real life, yet here was I – a child of television – performing in front of a *live* audience made up of those I loved most, who's approval I valued most. If I were to slip, stammer, trip or forget my lines I wouldn't be able to do the shot again and again until I got it right. I'd simply have to live with my first take.'

Martin decided to keep it simple. He avoided anecdotes, quotations and – adopting one rule from his television days – kept his alcohol intake to a minimum.

The speech was a great success and I'm sure his beautiful daughter, Melissa, will never forget it.

I'm grateful to Barry Cryer, Jimmy Tarbuck and Martin Bell M.P. for their excellent contributions. Stuart Turner, Peter Moloney, Rex Warner and Graham Davies are all represented by 'The Right Address', Britain's leading booking agency for after-dinner speakers. I extend my thanks to the agency and to their talented clients for the valuable help in my research.

Research and Development

If I had to compile a Top-Twenty of all speechmaking fears, the number one spot would definitely be: 'Do I have enough good material?'

In the midst of your heightening panic, it's possible that this particular anxiety may not have struck you as a 'biggie'. You've probably been quaking at the thought of facing an audience, stumbling over words, 'dying a death' and generally making a fool of yourself. However, most of these concerns point straight back to material – the content and quality of what you say.

I can tell you from my experience as a speechwriter, that when I read a completed speech to a nervous client, they laugh at the funny lines I've created for them, and their laughter is always a little louder than it should be. This is because their reaction has been fortified with sheer relief. They simply hadn't realised to what extent the material had been worrying them.

Now, however, when they hear the finished product, a load is instantly lifted and they actually begin to look forward to performing it themselves.

When I'm writing, either for myself or for a client, the first thing I need to do is look at the raw material of the assignment. Whether the subject of the speech is a person, an organisation or an ideal, my starting point is nearly always research.

We'll be examining three sources for that research:

◆ The use of 'allies'

◆ The Internet

◆ The printed word

RECRUITING 'ALLIES'

When it comes to inside information, there's no substitute for a good 'mole'.

You've been asked to make a speech at a friend's surprise birthday party but you haven't seen her for ages. You'd like to know some of the latest quirky things she gets up to these days. What she's like to live with. Does she still snore? Oh, and you've forgotten the town she was born in. Her husband, who's arranging the surprise, should immediately be appointed your official 'ally'. He'll have the answers you need.

You've been invited to reply on behalf of the guests at a Law Society Dinner. Your 'ally' is Sue Pickering – the organiser. She'll happily dish the dirt on the prominent members, the larger-than-life characters and any special guests.

Your reputation as a wit has lumbered you with having to make a speech at the Annual General Meeting of an associated company. You've spoken to a few of these people on the phone, but you know virtually nothing about them. Recruit the M.D.'s secretary immediately. What she doesn't know, she'll find out for you. And what she doesn't know about her boss, is almost certainly not worth knowing.

Contacts such as these are usually only too pleased to assist you with all kinds of valuable information at every stage of the process.

They'll arrange for a copy of the guest list, they'll pass on details of other speakers and interesting facts about any of the people you may wish to mention, they'll supply you with a profile of the company or association, they'll be able to brief you on current issues facing the industry and – at a later stage – help with travel arrangements, seating preferences, microphones and special equipment.

As you gather all this stuff from your 'allies', make sure you bear in mind how you'll be using this intelligence.

Leaving aside boring stuff like corporate policy and business matters, your 'allies' are of the greatest value when it comes to researching *people*. During your speech, you'll be roasting these characters – or at least making gentle, witty remarks about them – so you'll need to ask the right questions.

The questions you ask will, of course, depend on how well you already know the individual.

◆ What do they look like? Balding? Overweight? Bearded? (Wow! I don't like the sound of *that* girl!)

◆ Does he or she have a nickname?

◆ What about their education? Social background? Career background?

◆ Do they drink? Smoke? How heavily?

◆ Hobbies, Interests, Sports?

◆ Weaknesses, Eccentricities, Strange Habits?

◆ Family details: Single? Married? Divorced? Children? Details of parents.

As you will see in the next chapter, the important thing to remember about 'roast' material is that it has to have a ring of truth about it in order to be funny.

These jokes are verbal caricatures. They take a defect or a quirk and exaggerate it.

It's crucial, therefore, that the audience immediately recognises these foibles in your victim, so do make sure your 'ally' is a reliable source of information. Sometimes, certain characteristics passed on to you as part of a profile may affect only the person with whom you've been researching and could be quite obscure to others.

The M.D.'s secretary, for instance, may well see the guy as polite and quiet, whereas the rest of the world knows him to be a loud, arrogant yobbo. Needless to say, he's always on his best behaviour when dealing with someone so close to his boss, so she hasn't been allowed to see the prat as he really is.

It's your responsibility to make sure you get the character right. Persevere – ask and ask again. Ask other people if you can. You may get a different picture.

If you still have doubts, it's best to concentrate on the characteristics you're sure about.

Remember that your 'allies' are very close to their colleagues on a daily basis, and it's all too easy for them to neglect mentioning something they've known for some time and have become quite accustomed to. It may never occur to them to mention certain attributes or situations.

Of course, they could be withholding information in order to protect somebody's feelings. Someone like Graham King, for instance, recently cuckolded by a guy in the next department who was then swiftly transferred to the Botswana office.

They may not realise that keeping you in ignorance of this tricky situation runs the risk of your unintentionally causing embarrassment by making inappropriate jokes.

It's always a good idea to check with your 'allies' whether any of the people present have suffered recent trauma, serious injury, illness, or any other unfortunate experience where your material – however innocuous it may be – could cause pain or offence.

Imagine a young couple who suffered the recent loss of a child through cot death. If you were to go on and on about babies, you'd cause them discomfort at the very least.

A gag about a wooden leg would be less than tactful if there happened to be an amputee on the top table.

If you were to start riding the French a little too hard, that party of twenty from Lille may not feel so 'entente cordialish' at the end of the evening.

Your contact will not always volunteer this kind of information unless prompted, so be ready during the writing stage to get back to your 'ally' in the light of any material you feel could backfire.

Don't ever read them the lines, never give anything away. All you need to do is check out the lie of the land.

This kind of research shouldn't be taken to an extreme. You could drive yourself nuts trying to be all things to all people. If someone is all that distressed, they probably wouldn't be there in the first place. Just use your judgement and take into consideration how recently the trauma occurred and how the people concerned appear to handle the situation.

And remember this: the way you put your words together can make all the difference between funny and offensive.

THE INTERNET

I don't pretend to be an expert on the Internet, but I am finding it increasingly useful for the gathering of information.

As a research tool, it has a hell of a lot going for it; it's available twenty-four hours a day, it's world-wide, it's cheap, it's quite fast and all the information is there – if you can dig it out.

Here's how I use it to research.

Do I first need to explain what a Search Engine is?

Oh hell, I suppose so.

A Search Engine is a remotely accessible program that allows you to search for keywords on the Internet. There are many Search Engines available to you, free of charge. Each is a little different and you need to get the hang of which one works best for you.
You type in a word or phrase, and the program gathers up every reference it can find for you. It usually supplies you with a summary or an excerpt from the text of each of the sites in which this keyword is mentioned. You simply click on a 'link' alongside any reference that catches your eye, and you are automatically connected to the site itself.

Sometimes you can bite off a little more than you can chew. For instance, if you enter the word 'Golf', the Search Engine will present you with 3,817,110 matches!
Got a minute?

The trick is to refine your keywords so that the search results don't present you with long irrelevant listings.
Let's suppose you're the recently appointed captain of a golf club. By tradition, your club is hosting the region's annual greenkeepers dinner. These are the guys who maintain your course and keep it looking beautiful. As captain, you're naturally expected to say a few words of welcome and gratitude.

Trouble is, over the years you've taken their work very much for granted and know very little about their organisation or their aspirations. You can't ask anyone for information; you're supposed to know. You obviously need to research quietly and discreetly.

Sounds like a job for Captain Internet!

Let's choose a Search Engine. I rather like 'Alta Vista'. It's not all that fast during peak hours, but its database is pretty extensive.

If you remember, we tried entering 'Golf' and ended up with a grand total of 3,817,110 matches. If you were to start trawling through all that lot, you'd still be doing it when your *grandson* became captain, so we're going to have to narrow things down to a manageable level.

Let's see what happens when we enter 'greenkeeper'.

Click!

1005 matches found.

Now there's an improvement! Let's refine that a little. If we enter 'greenkeeper + golf' (ignore my inverted commas when entering), the Search Engine comes up with 8 matches, the first of which sounds most promising: it's a Website for 'Bigga' – the British And International Golf Greenkeepers Association. We click on the link and are connected to the site.
It's just one page of information, but it's a start. Print it out, or make some notes and continue.
This time, let's try 'greenkeeping + golf'. A subtle difference but you never know.

Click!

Nine matches, and one of the sites is dedicated to all greenkeepers and golf superintendents. It actually includes a Chat Room for golf course greenkeepers and several links to other similar sites.

Carry on looking into these pages, printing up as you go, and before too long, you'll have a pretty fair grounding in the subject.

The Internet, when used creatively, is capable of meeting most of your research needs, including funny material.

For some strange reason, millions of nerds love putting jokes on the Net, free of charge.

My advice? Help yourself in the name of research.

Enter 'Golf Jokes'

Click!

Result: 1,216,154 matches found.

Well, we're not going to be short of material, but we're going to have to work quite hard to choose it.

Fortunately, Search Engines are pretty intelligent and will normally place the most relevant content at the top of your results if you give them a few extra words to run with.

The downside of researching via the Internet is that you could easily find yourself playing on-line for hours if you don't exercise a certain amount of discipline. Don't *over*-research, it will encourage you to over-*write* and your speech will ramble on and on.

Be selective. Choose bits of information that really jump out at you and will sound good when spoken about.

THE PRINTED WORD

You wouldn't believe the state of my study when I'm writing. I'm always knee-deep in encyclopaedias, atlases, books of quotations, history books, biographical dictionaries, almanacs, joke books and word-finders. I also keep a pile of reference CD Roms next to my computer and scraps of paper all over my desk, so if you ever hear me emphasise the importance of organised working, don't believe me – it's utter bullshit.

The selection of reference books you'll want to have around depends, of course, on your usual speaking-topic.

If you make a lot of political speeches, for instance, you'll need publications like *The Oxford Dictionary of Political Quotations* and *Brewer's Politics*. If business is your thing, both Hutchinson and Collins produce dictionaries of business quotes. If you're into music, you may want *The Faber Companion To 20th Century Popular Music* (Phil Hardy and Dave Laing) on your shelf.

For the more formal speaker, *Debrett's Correct Form* is a *must*. It'll help with forms of address and precedence, and should protect you from slipping up where spoken etiquette is concerned.

Whitaker's Almanack could be described as a one-volume reference library. Published annually, the book is usually about thirteen hundred pages thick and covers subjects like Tidal Tables, Weights and Measures, Government Departments, Economic Statistics, The Media, Finance, Societies and Institutions and Countries of the World.

Do you ever get language blind spots?

Is it 'continuous' or 'continual'?
Specially or Especially?
Farther or Further?

There are several pocket guides to English Usage available and I urge you to get hold of one. Various editions are published by Newnes and Collins amongst (or is it among?) others.

These brilliant little books are compiled by very clever people who seem to know exactly where you're going to hit a problem, and provide you with examples of the correct way to utilise the alternatives.

English Dictionaries are easy. Just buy the best you can afford.

Encyclopaedias are a lot trickier but fortunately the famed *Encyclopaedia Britannica* is available on CD Rom nowadays, so this must be the way to go.

For certain personal speeches where a specific date is significant, such as birthdays, retirements, or reunions, you can add a nice extra touch by referring to news stories and world events which were taking place on or around that date.

This technique helps to create interesting pictures in the minds of your audience and places the subject into a chronological perspective.

A good source of this information is *Longman's Chronicle Of The 20th Century*. This large publication, prints and illustrates historical highlights of major events since 1900 in the form of newspaper style headlines. It updates annually.

I don't know about you, but I hate to hear the same word or phrase being used over and over again in a speech. Careless repetition is shoddy. It shows how little thought went into the process and quickly begins to distract an audience.

One way around this problem is to find synonyms for the repeating words.

When I was planning this book, I knew I would have to find a way to avoid mentioning the word 'fear' over and over again.

To the rescue came my trusty *Synonym Finder*, published by Rodale Press, a sort of sophisticated thesaurus.

I looked up 'fear' and discovered: anxiety, disquiet, dread, terror, panic, and many more useful alternatives.

I can tell you, I was really delighted: thrilled, joyous, happy, pleased, elated, ecstatic, gladdened ...

If you want to earn some of those extra audience points for topicality, please don't ignore the research potential of newspapers and magazines.

Although you can't be sure of a breaking news story until the day of the speech itself, you can still be ready with some material ahead of time. If a sporting event, a big trial or an election coincides with your speech date, prepare for all eventualities so that you have an appropriate gag ready, whatever the result.

Plan ahead, harness that information, and use it to your advantage.

Sooner or later, all the research material you've gathered together has to be converted into a format, capable of capturing interest, passing on information and, of course, entertaining.

There's no doubt about it, audiences crave humour in speeches.

They really lap it up.

An average one-liner based speech will often contain around forty-five gags, but relax, there's plenty of funny material around if you know where to look.

Over the years, I have built up a very large database of one-liners.

I'm therefore able to import as many of these lines as I need directly into the document I'm working on.

Chances are you don't yet have a database of gags, so you'll have to refer to one-liner books and other sources, and enter the material manually into your work document. Be very fussy. Choose only the best, the funniest. Choose with taste and restraint. Select lines that are easy to perform, easy to understand and will accurately hit the target.

No book on public speaking can ever be truly comprehensive. This one certainly isn't.
All I can do is pass on to you some of my own techniques and a personal perspective on speechwriting and public speaking.
However, there are many wonderful ideas and suggestions in other books and publications, so my final research suggestion is for you to get hold of one or two of the excellent titles available, each with their own point of view. Each designed to help you get an edge in wordwise.
They'll offer alternative suggestions, extra ideas and will probably confuse the hell out of you, but they're still worth buying.

I can highly recommend *The Public Speaker's Companion* by Stuart Turner, published by Thorsons, and – by the same author – *Public Speaking In Business* (McGraw Hill).

Every speaker should have a copy of *Just Say A Few Words* by the master himself Bob Monkhouse, published by Lennard.

An excellent source of well-chosen gags: *The Penguin Dictionary Of Jokes*, edited by Fred Metcalf.

Janner's Complete Speechmaker by Greville Janner, published by Business Books Ltd.

How To Write And Give A Speech by Joan Detz, published by St.Martin's Press.

For natty anecdotes on many subjects, *Podium Humor* and *More Podium Humor* by James C. Humes, published by Harper Perennial.

Finally, if you need what amounts to a ready-made printed database of inspired and useful one-liners, I can thoroughly recommend three books by a very promising kid:

Mitch Murray's One-Liners For Weddings

Mitch Murray's One-Liners For Business

and *Mitch Murray's One-Liners For Speeches On Special Occasions* – all published by Foulsham.

Writing that Speech

During my years as a songwriter, I made a wonderful discovery. I learned that it was only worth trying to write if I happened to be in the right frame of mind. If not, I'd be wasting my time. Anything I squeezed out of myself when I wasn't in the mood would be very ordinary indeed.

Okay, so it would be a well-constructed and tuneful composition with lyrics that sounded nice and made sense, but it wouldn't have any 'magic'.

Take my word for it, when you're trying to write a hit song – or anything else – 'magic' is the minimum requirement.

This discovery enabled me to be a hit songwriter with a *life*.

When it was time for me to work, I'd sit and mess around at the piano and if, after a while, nothing was happening creatively, I'd pour myself a drink and watch a Marx Brothers video, or go out and play poker, safe in the knowledge that I was not depriving the world of a classic hit song.

On the other hand, when I was inspired, I'd sit for hours, turning out as many bits and pieces as I could. I'd break the bones of an idea, then move on to another while I was still hot.

I could always come back and put the finishing touches to songs later during a less inspired writing session, but while I was buzzing, I'd go with the flow.

One sunny Sunday back in 1966, my good friends Barry Mason and Les Reed got together for a songwriting session at 9.30 in the morning. By 9 o'clock that night, they'd written the best part of seven songs, five of which ended up as international smash hits.

The Last Waltz became a Number One for Englebert Humperdink; *Delilah*, a Number One for Tom Jones; and *I Pretend*, another Number One for Des O'Connor. *Love Is All* was a Top Five hit for Malcolm Roberts, as was *Les Bicyclettes De Belsize* for Englebert.

A week earlier perhaps, the same two writers might have struggled all day and come up with nothing.

All this makes a total lie of the old saying, 'Creativity is ten per cent inspiration and ninety per cent perspiration'.
Trust me, it's the other way round.

So if, at any point, you find you seem to be struggling along, trying to compose a speech with just the right sparkle and it simply isn't happening, take time out; put the speech to one side and use that time to do some research or to gather more material.

THE STRATEGY

Let's begin by reminding ourselves of certain points I raised in earlier chapters.

◆ **Make it easy on yourself:** keep the speech short and simple, let it sound natural.

◆ **Think it through:** consider the setting, why you were chosen to speak, the aim of your speech, the composition of the audience, the time of day and any special circumstances you'll need to take into account.

◆ **Be choosy about the material you use:** select lines that sound good and arouse interest, avoid careless repetition, remember that most funny lines are based on truth, be tasteful and show restraint.

As you warm up your word processor, or gather your blank sheets of paper together ready to start writing, try to keep all these recommendations at the forefront of your mind, along with the general strategy of this – as yet – unborn speech.

Are you speaking to educate? To honour someone? To establish closer contacts? To raise money? To influence opinion?

Ninety per cent of the time the aim of the speech is clear. Occasionally, however, you'll find yourself in the situation of having to give a talk with no definable objective. Be aware that no matter how vague the assignment, you can't simply ramble on about nothing. If the speech has no raison d'être, contrive one: salute the organisation, propose a toast to absent friends, drink to the health of the chef. Anything.
This way, at least you have a starting point for your writing, and a subject to work with.

Mark Twain once said, 'It usually takes me more than three weeks to prepare a good impromptu speech.'
Never a man to be taken literally, old Mark was probably highlighting the painstaking effort involved in maintaining a casual approach to the text and delivery of his oratory.

(Personally, I preferred the work of Mark Twain's little-known brother – 'Choo Choo'.)

As you begin to write your speech, remember that the

wording must sound natural; don't say 'she is' when you'd normally say 'she's', don't say 'I am' when you'd normally say 'I'm', don't say 'you will', say 'you'll' unless, of course, you're deliberately emphasising the word 'will' as in 'You *will* tell your friends about this book, won't you?'

Use normal language, not pseudo 'speech-talk'. Write your speech in language that will sound almost conversational, and won't flaunt the fact that you're reading it.

A good speech, like a good song, needs a regular beat. It should have a rhythm of its own: peaks, troughs, crescendos and a climax.

(Don't you love it when I talk dirty?)

Think about the character of your speech. Is it a ballad, or is it rock and roll?

Consider these factors:

◆ What time of the day is it?

◆ What is the size and composition of your audience?

◆ What's the nature of your message?

Choose and construct your material to harmonise with the circumstances, and the rhythm of your speech, along with its highs and lows, will happen almost automatically.

Your form of delivery, the style of material and the amount of material you use, will – to a great extent – depend on the clock.

◆ Early morning?

Their funny bones are still asleep.

Keep it simple and businesslike; morning humour should be restricted to the occasional quip or witty comment.
Nothing too subtle. Nothing too long. Nothing contrived.

◆ After lunch?

Loosen up. They're ready.
They've eaten, they've sipped a little wine, they've chatted.
They're warmed up.

Warning: Don't overdo it if this is a business presentation. The day's still young and there's too much work ahead to be flippant.

◆ After dinner?

The traditional time for brandy, cigars and laughter.
People are receptive to a little entertainment immediately after the meal.
They're laid-back, mellow, relaxed.
Okay, let's face it – they're pissed!

If you have any say in the programme, don't leave it too long before you speak or your audience will start to become impatient or unruly or over-tired or aggressive – or any combination of the above.
If this happens, you'll have to revert to your early morning approach and cut the speech by two thirds.

(I'm ever so pleased I won't be there.)

Don't try to be too businesslike when your speech is made in the after-dinner slot; at that time, the atmosphere is one of informality, and too much emphasis on company matters won't go down very well.

Treat your after-dinner talk as a quasi-social speech and construct it accordingly.

STRUCTURE

There's a traditional speechwriting method which has now become something of a cliché but remains sound advice – particularly for business speeches:

1 Tell 'em what you're going to tell 'em
2 Tell 'em
3 Tell 'em what you told 'em

The structure of a social speech is not all that different from that of a business speech or presentation, but it does tend to be more linear, so 'Tell 'em what you told 'em' rarely applies. It's not imperative to remind your listeners of the main points. You merely end with a toast which rounds things off quite nicely.

In either form, your topic or proposition is, of course, central to the talk, but your audience shouldn't be expected to focus on it indefinitely. As I've said before, modern-day speechmaking can only ever be an exercise in superficiality. We've all been conditioned by the media to absorb soundbites, and are rapidly becoming unable to tolerate anything more substantial. As you can imagine, this puts one hell of a strain on those soundbites. They have to be pretty damn good.

They also have to appear justifiable within the context of the speech, and that's why – later – I'm going to be setting out a few rules for their selection and use.

Think of the speech you are about to write, as a wheel. The hub of that wheel is the topic of the speech, the spokes are issues and characters.

As you deal with issues, or have fun with characters, you'll need to make frequent trips back to the hub in order to keep the speech on track.

This way, the wheel keeps rolling as you manoeuvre within it.

THE OPENING

On nearly every occasion, a good opening is crucial. It's designed to loosen the collars, set the mood and begin the action.

It's the speaker's way of saying, 'Don't worry folks, this speech is not going to be as boring as you thought.'

Effective openers are like gold dust. They hand you a valuable psychological advantage. If you can kick-start your audience into awarding you an early laugh or some kind of positive reaction, fear immediately becomes a non-issue and you begin to relax and enjoy your own performance.

Every laugh or giggle strengthens you. You suddenly find you're tossing in off-the-cuff comments, conducting the audience like a symphony orchestra, and by the end of the speech you'll be a bloody little hero.

That's how crucial a good opening can be.

Some of the finest speechmakers like to open with an anecdote. An anecdote can be an ideal link into the theme of your presentation. If chosen carefully, a good opening story will illustrate your topic or indicate exactly where you stand on a subject.

Even I – a confirmed one-liner man – have to admit that an effective anecdote can be an excellent way to launch a speech.

However, for the terrified speaker this kind of opening

presents an unacceptable risk.

There's really no shortage of books packed with amusing stories suitable for speechmakers. Once you develop your skills, you may well feel brave enough to give anecdotes a try. Until then, don't gamble with that all-important opening.

WHO THE HELL ARE YOU?

Your next priority is to establish your credentials.

It's disconcerting and distracting for an audience to remain unaware of the background or potential agenda of the speaker.

Even if you have just been introduced by a toastmaster or an M.C., it's useful for people to know a little more.

You only need use a few words to make your point:

◆ **When I was first elected to serve as a
  magistrate in this area ...**

◆ **Being Creative Director on this project, I've
  been asked to ...**

◆ **As the bridegroom's step-brother ...**

You could actually combine an opening line with your credentials, and earn yourself a little laugh:

**Good evening ladies and gentlemen, I'm Howard
Nicholls – the Society's Chief Accountant. I'm
here to help you through your after-dinner nap.**

Once you gain a little more experience as a speaker, you may develop the knack of inspiring a certain amount of blind acceptance of your authority. This will give you enough flexibility to delay your self-justification until a little later in the speech. However, for the time being, plan on establishing your credentials at a very early stage.

Now, you may feel this 'credentials' stuff is unnecessary in a family gathering, and much of the time you'll be right, but even in a wedding situation you have to reckon that about half the guests won't know who you are, or what relationship you have with the person you're speaking about. To get maximum reaction, your audience will need to know where you fit into the picture.

There are times when you need to establish your credentials in order to justify ribbing others.
No audience will grant you the right to make fun of a virtual stranger. Under these circumstances, even words of mild mockery will sound highly insulting.
Letting the audience know that you are close friends with your 'victim', allows them to enjoy the roast without having to feel protective or embarrassed.

WHAT'S THE POINT?

Having established your credentials, you are now ready to introduce your topic, if you have one.

Try to find an intriguing way of doing this. Arouse their curiosity. Ask a silly question perhaps:

Topic: Textiles

When it rains, why is it that sheep don't shrink?

Topic: Conservation

What do you do when you see an endangered animal eating an endangered plant?

Topic: Investment

How did the fool and his money ever get together in the first place?

Topic: Careers

Apparently, there are over four hundred sexual positions ... but here's the big question: where do you apply for them?

From here, link to your topic by saying something like:

Well, I'm afraid the answer to that will have to remain one of life's great mysteries, but it does raise an interesting point ...

You may prefer something less surreal. Find something connected to your topic to stimulate the interest of your audience. Think of an angle few would have even considered:

Have you ever wondered what Bernard Matthews does with all those turkey feathers?

The purpose of introductions such as these – factual or silly – is to plant pictures in the mind and excite the imagination.
Once you've grabbed their attention, chances are they'll buy a ticket and hop on board.

Okay, you've opened the speech, established your credentials and introduced your topic.

I simply can't put this off any longer – I'm now going to have to lay down the law:

ONE-LINERS – THE RULES

The one-liner construction has a lot going for it; the rhythm is simple to maintain, your investment shows a return every seven or eight seconds and the format creates the illusion of a shorter, snappier speech – very handy if you're not exactly an experienced orator.

If a joke or a comment falls flat, so what?
You're straight into the next line and, chances are, nobody will even notice that your one-liner didn't work.
On the other hand, the longer story or anecdote is an investment which *has* to pay off. If a thirty-second story dies a death, you have a real problem!

We've all suffered the bloke who genuinely thinks he's a raconteur but in reality couldn't tell the difference between a comma and a coma!

In the context of an otherwise serious speech, one-liners bring a sense of proportion to issues, help the audience to concentrate on the subject and enhance the general charisma of the speaker.

Using these little sound-splashes selectively, will help remove that air of pomposity, intensity and desperation which – believe me – is very off-putting to an audience.

Before we come to the rules, please bear in mind that I'm using the term 'one-liners' in a very generalised way; sometimes you'll be using two or three-line gags, sometimes the one-liner won't be a funny line at all – it could even be a sentimental comment or a piece of prose.

My God! Is that the time? I don't believe it – it's time for the rules.

RULE No. 1

Make sure the one-liners you select are entirely appropriate for your audience and suitable for your style of delivery.

I am in the presence of my audience long before I arrive at the venue. In my imagination, the crowd is listening to me as I *write*.
I picture how many people are present, their likely mood, their social mix and average age. I consider my placement within the running-order of the programme and try to take on board the likely effect of earlier speakers and their varying styles.

The way you word your speech depends to a large extent upon the size and demeanour of your audience. If you are speaking to a small group of nineteen, your words will be quite different from those you'd use when facing a gathering of a hundred and ninety. Your language would be more intimate, your gestures more subtle. Equally, a boozy, rowdy crowd of pissheads would have to be addressed by 'one of the boys'. (Good luck with *that* lot, mate!)

When it comes to one-liners, integrity is everything.

Almost any speech or presentation is bound to benefit greatly from the skilful use of quips or gags, provided the humour is carefully customised and in character.
When you're choosing lines and wording your speech, consider whether you have enough perceived 'clout' to put certain lines across.

As I warned earlier in the book, you may well be too *young* to get away with a particular quip, whereas a seasoned speaker would bring the house down with it. From you, it could sound impudent, but they'd take it from him.

Several years ago, someone published a book highlighting the wit of Prince Phillip. At face value, most of the lines were pretty ordinary. Slightly amusing at best. However, when you began to imagine these words coming from the lips of the Queen's husband, they became hilarious. A few run-of-the-mill comments suddenly adopted a magnificent irreverence when attributed to His Royal Highness The Duke of Edinburgh, and that made them funny.

Most of Tommy Cooper's silly throw-away lines only come to life when you picture that face and remember the way he delivered them.

Humour, like music, is very often a package deal. The combination of Nat King Cole and that fabulous song, *The Touch Of Your Lips*, is pure magic. No question. But take exactly the same song, record it with Rolf Harris and the effect would be horrifyingly different.

(Don't do it, Rolf!)

RULE No.2

Don't contrive an attribute or a situation in order to justify using a one-liner, no matter how funny you think it is.

As I keep telling you, one-liners have to have an obvious ring of truth in order to be funny. These jokes are verbal caricatures.

They take a physical characteristic or an idiosyncrasy and exaggerate it.
This doesn't mean you can't lie – you could place the victim in a country he's never visited, as long as it's reasonably feasible and won't be taken literally. You could tell porkies about a conversation you had with the chairman before dinner, you could invent a sexual

deviation or a secret talent. However, you need to guard against any distraction liable to come between the audience and the gag. If a guy is of average build, don't try making 'fatty' jokes. You'll confuse the customers.

If, however, he's obviously overweight, go ahead: make him as big as a house if you want to, providing he can take it and that you're sure the audience won't squirm with embarrassment on his behalf.

RULE No. 3

Don't screw around too much with one-liners.

Certain words which may appear innocuous or superfluous, could be part of the magic that makes us laugh. Removing those words, or changing their position may be fatal to the line.
Think very carefully before making any substitution; even if you've come up with something you feel is better, it may not be funnier.

Some words are simply funny words.
For example:

'Hen' – nothing,   'Chicken' – funny.

'Gloves' – nothing,   'Socks' – funny.

'Beige' – nothing,   'Puce' – funny.

The expression 'Father-in-law' is not in the least funny, whereas 'Mother-in-law' is absolutely side-splitting.

At least, it would be if it wasn't so tragic!

Don't impede the subtle psychology of a joke by padding it out. The element of surprise is highly important in humour. One-liners usually contain a 'set-up' and a 'sting'. For example:

Set up: **I'd love to see her in something long and flowing ...**

Sting: ... **like a river!**

The words 'long and flowing' are crucial. They conjure up the image of a beautiful ball gown. The audience has been 'set up' for the surprise of the 'sting' line. Change these words and you lose the point. Put a line or even a word between 'flowing' and 'river' and you weaken the impact. Your audience has to retain the memory of the 'set up' in order to realise they've been had.

So don't be tempted to embellish a good line.

If it ain't broke, don't fix it!

Equally, if you feel you need to trim a one-liner, make sure that your cut doesn't damage the flow. Sometimes a gag can sound 'one-legged' if the rhythm is disturbed.

The following example may help to reinforce your understanding of how a joke is digested.

Set up: **Earlier this evening, at the reception, I met Gerry Marshall; a brilliant lawyer and a real gentleman ...**

Sting: ... **later on I had drinks with all three of them!**

The audience readily, but mistakenly, takes on board what they believe is your description of Gerry Marshall.

Suddenly, they hear the words: 'all three of them'.

They rewind to 'Gerry Marshall, a brilliant lawyer and a real gentleman', and realise you've conned 'em.

Incidentally, with this style of one-liner, you have to allow for a couple of extra beats before you get your laugh; the thought process often produces a delayed reaction.

Now, I don't want to give you the impression that there's always a logic to comedy. There isn't.

The hyena eats once a day, and mates once a year ... What the hell has *he* got to laugh about?

No logic, see?

Take Henny Youngman ... please! (Oh, I forgot ... God already did.)

Henny Youngman is known as America's 'King Of The One-Liners'. Here's one of his famous gags:

> **You know, there's nothing like getting up at six in the morning, putting on a pair of shorts, jumping into the sea, swimming out five miles and then swimming back.**
>
> **There's nothing like it, so why do it?**

It gets a big laugh every time, but why? If you tried to dissect it, you'd get nowhere.

The joke is funny all right, but it doesn't make sense.

There's nothing like it ... This means it's a unique experience.

So why do it? Why not? People go to a lot of trouble to enjoy a unique experience.

Perhaps the laugh comes as a result of the slim excuse and flawed logic the portly comedian is offering to justify his preference for the sedentary life.

Who knows? Who cares – it works.
Be happy for Henny.

I hate analysing comedy – it really ruins it. A line is either funny or it isn't, so I'm very sorry, I really must apologise for having to get into all this.

On the other hand, sometimes an illustration or two may help someone avoid ruining an otherwise effective line and I'm the one landed with the responsibility of pointing you in the right direction.

It's a dirty job, but somebody's got to do it, so to hell with it – I withdraw my apology!

As you glance through the various gags and quips listed in this book and others, you may find that many of the lines need to be read aloud before you see the joke.

This illustrates how important it is to remember that you are writing for the *ear*, not for the eye.

Don't forget, your audience will be listening, not reading.

PEOPLE

Everybody's favourite kind of speech is one bursting at the seams with people.

An audience loves being brought into the action. They enjoy hearing about themselves, their colleagues, their friends. They love you for having the guts to make fun of the pompous, they admire you for being clever about the stupid and for being stupid about the clever. They appreciate the obvious effort you've put into the speech, and they feel flattered you've devoted so much time in order to entertain them.

Right then, let's start baking our people pie.

If you haven't done so already, make a list of all those you'll be referring to, along with details of their occupations, appearance, personality traits, eccentricities and other qualities.
It may be one person, it may be seven. The same advice applies.

Check out the corresponding one-liners and select one or two of the funniest for each of the characteristics you wish to highlight.
Don't overdo it. You don't need to mention everybody present. What you will need, however, is a device to justify naming names and talking about them.

Try these:

> I was having a chat a little earlier this evening with Craig Perriman, and he was telling me what a boring table he was on ...
> and I thought to myself, how lucky I am to be sitting with such a great load of characters ...
> people like ...

Or:

> I must say I'm not really sure why you'd want to hear about me when there are so many other more interesting characters here this evening; people like ...

As you list jokes about their little quirks or weird hobbies or social behaviour, keep one eye on the topic of the speech and look for opportunities to bounce some of these one-liners back to it.

In the case of the retiree, for instance, you could make fun of his disastrous attempts at 'home-improvement', then return to the topic by speculating on the havoc he will wreak now that he has so much more time on his hands.

In the anniversary speech, joke about the husband's endless golf jaunts over the years, then return to the topic by complimenting his long-suffering wife on handling the situation so well.

In the best man's speech, gloat at the curtailment of the bridegroom's former activities now that he's wearing a ring – through his nose.

Once you have re-established the topic, you are free to wander back into one-liner land again, this time featuring a different character or issue.

You don't have to return to the hub of your speech-wheel after every character you mention. You could link directly from one person to another before returning to your topic. The lines you use should bridge to each other as naturally as possible with a logical pattern.

If you intend to start off with a few general roast lines about a bridegroom, for instance, progress to gags about the size of your victim's ears, then to the amount he drinks, into his reputation as a womaniser (careful!) linking to the way he met his bride, how wonderful she is, some nice lines about her, then maybe some stuff on the two of them together.

Your aim is to end up with a cleverly crafted succession of strong one-liners in a natural, flowing format.

Don't worry. You can do it. Lean on me.

Ow!

EDITING AND BRIDGING

One of the many great benefits of the one-liner format is the freedom it gives you to edit 'on site' or in real time.
This structure makes it remarkably easy to remove lines and close up the gaps.
Suppose someone you intended to welcome hasn't turned up; simply skip that part of the speech and carry on with the next segment.

If, despite your personality and witty presentation, you begin to sense that the audience has had enough, it's a simple matter to cut from where you are to a later section, or even straight to the close of the speech.
See my section on 'Closing Your Speech', and I'll show you how to get away with it.

With our one-liner construction, the omissions shouldn't affect the flow. Most of the lines are self-contained; if you've planned on doing two or three one-liners about your Scottish Office Supervisor's healthy ego and you feel the speech is dragging at that point, just use the best one.

Make sure, however, that your link words are suitable and are not too repetitive.

So now you're thinking 'What the hell are 'link words'?'

Right?

You see, I knew exactly what you were thinking.
We authors are very clever people.

'Link words' are what I call the little spoken punctuations and phrases used to move from one line to another; words like 'Now ... ', 'Nevertheless ... ', 'You know ... ', 'Mind you ... ', 'After all ... ', 'In any case ... '

Simply reciting pages of one-liners without the use of link words wouldn't work in a speech. You need them in order to bond your lines together, thereby creating the illusion of a natural progression.
Don't forget, you're coming out of a laugh into the next gag, and it's more impressive for the audience to feel their laughter has forced you to pause than for you to appear as if you're throwing lines at them and hoping for the best.

You also need to 'bridge' from one subject to another in order to maintain a smooth and logical flow.

In the following example, I'll be making several points about my victim, I'll be using 'link words' (underlined), and I'll be 'bridging' from subject to subject straight into the closing of my speech.

All this while drinking a glass of water.

What a man!

The 'victim' is Stuart Reid – a timber merchant.
He's decided to take 'Late Retirement' and this speech is being made at his farewell party.
We cover his pathetic attempts at keeping fit, his enthusiasm for alcohol, his admiration for the opposite sex, his shaky medical profile and – the dominant theme – his advanced years.

Poor sod.

We join the speech three quarters of the way through:

> ... **by the way**, I happen to know that last month,
> Stuart went out and bought eight 'Men's Health'
> magazines, six general fitness publications,
> four manuals on exercise and a medical
> encyclopedia ...
> They had an influence on his health all right ...
> while he was carrying them out to the garage, he
> ruptured himself!
> **Nevertheless**, he still takes fitness quite
> seriously; at home, he even has his own parallel
> bars ...
> One for brandy, one for scotch!
>
> *(Bridging line)*

> **Okay**, so Stuart Reid enjoys a drink ... what's
> wrong with that?

> **To be fair**, he's cut down quite a bit; this guy
> used to drink so much gin, Gordon's thought he
> was a wholesaler!

> ... but recently, one of his many lady friends told
> him he was like a load of fireworks in November
> ... bloody useless after the fifth!
>
> *(Bridging line)*

> **Funnily enough**, it's just been announced that, to
> coincide with Stuart's retirement, they're going
> to be hanging his zip in the Timber Merchant's
> Hall of Fame.

> **Oh yes**, Stuart was always quite a ladies man.

> **Mind you**, the only hot number he's into these
> days is his blood pressure!
>
> *(Bridging line)*

There was a time, when he was younger, he'd do anything to go out with a nurse ...
Nowadays, of course, he daren't go out with<u>ou</u>t a nurse!

Never mind Stuart, there's good news ...
according to current medical opinion, there's no reason you shouldn't be able to enjoy sex past ninety ...
as long as you let somebody else drive!

Ladies and gentlemen ... despite his age, Stuart Reid has quite a lot going ...
his hair's going, his teeth are going, his liver's going ...
Come to think of it, *I'd* better be going! I've only got three minutes left and I usually need that for applause ... so please join me in drinking a toast to ...

The above example illustrates how to bridge from subject to subject, and demonstrates the use of link words, not only for the purpose of joining lines together in a natural way, but also to alert your audience to the next line, and often to qualify it.

By the way, a bridging line doesn't necessarily have to be funny in itself. All it needs to do is help you get from one subject to another. It may be a straight statement, a play on words or any other device capable of making the transition appear seamless.

Some people say Reg is lazy ... this is most unfair;

I know he had his window box paved over, but what does that prove?

<u>Naturally</u> he's well aware that hard work never *killed* anyone ... but he's certainly not going to take any chances on being its first victim.

<u>In fact</u>, he's stopped drinking coffee in the morning; it keeps him awake for the rest of the day!

<u>Mind you</u>, he isn't lazy when it comes to playing golf ...

(Bridging line)

now there's one activity where he can certainly hold his own ...
of course, this doesn't make it any easier to hit the ball.

Reg is not the kind of plumber who takes Wednesdays off to play golf. Not Wednesdays! ... that's the day he works!

You'll notice that at times, it sounds as if you are defending the victim.
However, this 'defence' is merely a device which gives you the excuse to continue laying into him.

I call it 'Safe Slander', and you'll find more on this in the next section.

> In the selection of one-liners included in this book, most of those suitable for bridging from one subject to the next will be specially indicated.
> The subsequent subject will usually be quite obvious.
> With a little imagination, however, you'll be able to bridge from many others.

MAKING THE MOST OF A ROAST

I know I keep banging on about this truth stuff, so I think I owe it to you to further justify my case.

If, for instance, your Company Secretary is a little – how can I put it? – unexciting (a fanciful thought, I know, but let's hypothesise), you may well say:

> **Ladies and gentlemen, some people need no introduction ...**
> **Brian Torrance needs all the introduction he can get.**
>
> **Once seen, never remembered, Brian has that magic ability to light up a room ... as soon as he leaves it.**
>
> **He's never had a very high profile ... in fact, the monogram on his shirt says: 'occupant' ...**

and so on ...

But would that material be funny if – despite his profession – Brian Torrance was known to be a hyperactive, colourful dude and the life-and-soul of the party?

Of course not.

The audience laughs at the parody of what it recognises as Brian's insipid disposition.
All your roast lines need to have this kind of credibility; the stronger the characteristic, the more effective the routine will be.

For instance, if you're going to laugh at his drinking, make sure he drinks for England and is not just a 'white wine with a meal' man.

Only one thing takes priority over truth: audience perception.

Let's say a guy in the office, perhaps because of his shyness, has an undeserved reputation as an intellectual lightweight.
Even though you happen to know that he's really very bright indeed, you must make jokes on the basis of the way people see him rather than focus your humour on the true situation as only you know it.

If you can't stomach making yourself party to a misconception of this kind, don't joke about him at all.
Try to hit the button when you roast, but don't be too cruel. Even if the roastee is liable to take it well, many members of the audience are going to be concerned for your victim's feelings if you cross that sensitive line.
Think about the person you wish to rib; you may find something in his (never *her*) appearance – shortish, big nose, beer belly?
Is he an insensitive boor? A mummy's boy? A dirty old man?
I hope so. All that makes for a much better speech.

The ideal subject for a roast is an *equal*. Someone of exactly the same status. As long as he can put up with a put-down, you'll have no problem at all.
However, if you want to roast someone you are supposed to treat with a certain amount of deference – a corporate superior, or your new wife's father, for instance – watch it, chum.
Don't be misled by the easy-going personal manner they may seem to have in private; there is a big difference between one-to-one banter and public ribbing.
Personally, they may not be offended, but they could start

to worry about the reactions of others who may be embarrassed on their behalf.

Making jokes at the expense of corporate 'underlings' should be treated with as much care and trepidation as you would apply when cracking gags about superiors.
Don't bully, don't humiliate. The victim won't find it funny and the audience will cringe.

There's another reason to be gentle with your subordinate: One day that spotty little sod may be promoted above you in the company hierarchy, and overnight you may find yourself up a quaintly named creek without any means of propulsion.

It simply ain't worth it.

Bearing all this in mind, wouldn't it be useful to be equipped with a brilliant technique guaranteed to help you navigate that treacherous channel between sycophancy and insubordination?
Well, ain't you the lucky reader?

Allow me to introduce my latest dirty trick. A fiendish ruse designed to give you the benefit of the jokes whilst shielding you from too much responsibility.

I think this calls for a small ceremony:

> *I name this schtick 'SAFE SLANDER'.*
> *May God bless it, and all who assail with it.*

The idea of 'Safe Slander' is to attack the ugly things people say about the subject of your roast.
You appear to defend the victim and side with him in outrage. This way, although you distance yourself from the sentiment, you still pick up all the laughs.

You may wish to adopt these principles in order to distance yourself from the directness of the material, but don't kid yourself that you'll be fooling anyone. It's just that, with a protective extra psychological tier, you have a better chance of getting away with it.

And if you understood that last line, you obviously don't get out enough.

Here are some 'Safe Slander' techniques in action:

> ... People say he has a personality problem. I don't know what they're talking about ...
> Who started the rumour that when he was in Canada, a load of baby seals got together and clubbed *him*?!
>
> How stupid! ...
>
> Why do people spread these silly stories?
>
> They say he climbed a mountain in Switzerland, called out 'Hello!', and the echo said: 'Jump!'
>
> It's not true, it's not nice, it's not fair!

You may even mildly rebuke the audience for dignifying these scandalous rumours with laughter.

> Why are you laughing? We're talking about a man's reputation here!
> Do you think it's funny?! Do you think it's right that people should say he's the only man in history ever to be told by Mother Theresa to 'Piss off!'? ...
>
> Give the guy a break.

(Make sure you follow this routine with a smile; we don't want to confuse anybody.)

AVOIDING STORIES

Occasionally, you'll find that an incident or an amusing episode has recently occurred and you're expected to make some mention of it in your speech.

I'd strongly advise you against repeating the whole story (unless your name is Peter Ustinov).

As an experience, it may have been funny if you were there at the time, but as part of an otherwise fast-moving speech, you risk losing your audience.

The trick is merely to allude to the event by using an appropriate one-liner.

For instance, let's assume it's common knowledge that Andy, one of your pals with a reputation for fast and scary driving, recently managed to spin his Audi off the road.

No need to relate the whole incident, one gag will do the job:

> **You may have noticed Andy Wilson's car parked outside ...**
> **It's a very unusual motor ... it has four headlights, two radiators, and the engine's in the back.**
>
> **... of course it wasn't always like that ... only since the accident.**

If your chief planning officer tripped and tumbled down the steps of the Town Hall, you only have to remind people of:

... **the day Richard Cowley re-discovered gravity.**

Get the picture?

Here's another thought on one-liners: as you happily sit around selecting little 'take-the-pissiles', make absolutely certain that none of the lines you're using against your victims, apply equally to you.

If the Post Office recently gave your nose its own postcode, don't bother to make cracks about someone with a big schnozz.

If you're so thin that Steve Davis keeps chalking your head, don't try to roast that skinny guy in Credit Control.

If your teeth protrude so much that when you smile you comb your beard, don't waste your time joking about the General Manager's overbite!

Hey ... I've just pictured you.

Urghhh!

Of course, there's nothing wrong in roasting *yourself*. It's great fun and it can be rather endearing, if you don't take it too far:

> I think I should point out that I do have a slight speech impediment. I'm telling you this in case I happen to stumble on the occasional word this evening ... but really, there's very little ch ... ch ... ... chance of that happening.

> You know, I had a cousin with the same problem ... a really bad stammer. He joined the parachute regiment. They told him to count to three and pull the rip cord ... I'm really going to miss him.

If you're bandaged up, or if your leg is in a cast:

> **Well, this proves it – you always hurt the one you love.**

If you're a big guy:

> **My wife's a weight-watcher ... she's watched mine go from ten stone to fourteen stone six!**

This next line will kill two birds with one stone; it makes a nice self-basting roast, and it leads you neatly into zapping the others:

> **Of course, it has to be admitted that the guys on the committee have a serious judgement problem ... after all, they were the ones who invited me to speak tonight, so that'll give you some idea.**

THE 'PING PONG' PRINCIPLE

Every now and then you may be called upon to shower praise upon a colleague, an associate or a well-respected member of the family.
He or she may be retiring, marrying, receiving an award, moving in, moving up, moving on, or even being buried.

From an early age, we British are urged to keep a stiff upper lip. By implication, therefore, we're allowed to let the lower one go limp.
Is it any wonder that some of us have trouble being understood?

More to the point, unlike our American cousins, we are not very comfortable using gushing, extravagant language when praising individuals.

That's our problem; our inhibitions and hang-ups are often liable to endanger the expression of our genuine feelings.

In short, sometimes sincerity just doesn't ring true.

We all know many genuine people who simply can't help sounding like phoneys; it's the language they use and the tone they adopt.

In a tribute speech, it can be quite difficult to maintain the balance between flowery, sentimental schmaltz and cold formality. You need to let your audience know how much you admire the subject of your speech, yet, if you overdo the superlatives, the crowd is liable to start throwing up en-masse.

In the family setting, this problem particularly affects the father of the bride, who has to demonstrate to his guests and relatives how much he cares for his little darling, but doesn't want to sound too much like a big Jessie.

The corporate world raises some challenging considerations of its own.
If you're a manager paying tribute to one of your staff, you'll want to avoid any charge of favouritism.
You can't risk downgrading the rest of the team by implication. And remember, the human body is strange; occasionally, too much patting on the back will result in a swollen head!

All in all, a tribute speech has to be a fine balancing trick.

Make sure you avoid being too nice for too long. Alternate your sincere observations with little bits of mischievous humour.

I call this style 'The Ping Pong Principle'.

The 'Ping Pong Principle' works like this:
You praise ... you sting.
You acclaim ... you knock.
You toast ... you roast.

For example, here's a lighthearted 'softener' you could use
in order to break up the monotony of continuous praise.
Insert the line either exactly as it is, or adapt it to the world
of sport, politics, or voluntary work:

> **As if all these achievements weren't enough, in
> his lifetime this man has also made a major
> contribution to the St. John Ambulance Brigade
> ... he stayed out of it.**

From here, swiftly move back to positive humour:

> **But we're lucky to have him ... he's brilliant!
> His I.Q. is higher than Ian Paisley's blood
> pressure.**

Ping! Break again:

> **Yes, Bill Huntley is a great organiser, he's warm,
> he's intelligent, he's ...
> Sorry Bill, I can't read your writing, what does
> that say? ...
> Oh yes ... 'modest'.**

Pong! – Back to positive humour:

> **A lot of people are surprised that Bill is a friend
> of Cabinet Ministers, top entertainers, royalty ...
> but why not? – Even *they* need someone to look
> up to.**

... and so on.

How about our father of the bride?

As the welcoming host, he can hardly avoid paying tribute to his lovely daughter (even if she's a bow wow) and his guests will have to tolerate his performance, good or bad, in return for all the free food and booze.
Nevertheless, it's his daughter's big day, and he mustn't let her down. He's expected to say a few reasonably sober, sensitive yet witty words.

He also has to include some love and affection.
Now that takes sincerity, and sincerity's a right pain in the arse – and I mean that most sincerely.

> It's inevitable, I suppose, that a day like today inspires a few memories ... in particular, memories of this young bride's formative years.

> You know, when Lucille was born, she looked exactly like me ... then they turned her the right way up and all was well.

> People think of my daughter as a very bright young lady, and so she is, but we weren't too sure when she was younger. At kindergarten, Lucy was different from all the other five year olds ... she was eleven!

> And I have to admit that even at Victoria College she was not the brightest of pupils ... one day in the assembly hall she saw a sign saying: 'Wet Floor' ... so she did!

> At one stage, I had my doubts about the crowd she was hanging around with ... I used to have to pay her pocket money in unmarked bills!

But our Lucy was never any trouble at home. She
was a quiet girl.
Every now and then, I'd glance up at the shelf
and there she'd be ... sitting there ... waiting ...

Thankfully, today marks the end of that waiting
and I know that Lucy feels that Dave has been
well worth waiting for.

He is, after all, a fine young man with many
interests ... he's into sailing and golf and, so far,
his progress in the world of business has been
meteoric.

I'm confident that my daughter is in good hands;
after all, show me a man with both feet on the
ground, and I'll show you a man who ... can't
put his trousers on!

Dave, you certainly seem to know how to make
Lucy happy and I'm quite sure you'll continue to
do so.

Welcome to the family ... and believe me, you
are welcome to the bloody family!

I think you'll find that Lucy is going to be an
asset to you in all sorts of ways ...

She's quite a career girl herself and, even though
a father shouldn't really say it, Lucille has
everything it takes to be a success in business ...
a quiet charm, a persuasive manner, the ability
to grovel without laddering her tights ...

See what I mean?

First sweet, then zap! First this way, then that.
Ping Pong.

> Another good thing about the Ping Pong
> method is that the audience doesn't want to
> miss the next one-liner, so they actually
> concentrate – in much the same way as you
> can't put this book down because I'm so
> bloody hilarious!

TASTE AND RESTRAINT

Unless you're speaking to a load of 'born again' fanatics,
you don't have to go out of your way to make your speech
as pure as the driven snow. On the contrary, if you don't
have just a little slush, many audiences may even regard
you with suspicion.

In most settings nowadays, you can get away with fairly
risqué material, but never be too vulgar; avoid being
'lavatorial' and try to be subtle with sexual references.

For most occasions, apart from stag nights, the serious
four-letter words are definitely taboo, of course. However,
provided you use them only occasionally and advisedly,
words like 'pissed', 'bullshit', 'crap', and 'bonk' are all
right in the correct context.

(Out of context, they'll sound as stark as they did in the
previous paragraph, so watch it!)

Some lines actually depend on a rude word for maximum
impact – that element of naughtiness gives the line an
extra humorous edge. Not always, but more often than
you'd think.

As an example, take these two definitions:

> **The ideal legal client is a very wealthy man in deep shit!**

> **The ideal legal client is a very wealthy man in a great deal of trouble!**

The first version will produce a belly laugh, the second will bring forth a genial, knowing giggle. Nevertheless, by changing the 'deep shit' ending, the line has not been killed; it's still worth using. You just have to accept that by toning down the language you've toned down the reaction. There are, of course, all sorts of substitutions you could use but please be aware that certain one-liners are useless without the ripe language; they lack a certain vital eloquence.

Some years ago, when a famous recording star turned down one of my songs on the grounds that he didn't believe it would sell, I could easily have shrugged it off like a good sport and thanked him for listening.
But just imagine how much more impact was created by the colourful observation I actually made at the time, namely: 'You wouldn't know a hit song if it flew up your arse and bit your liver!'

Cliff turned to religion shortly afterwards.

Use your common sense, select every one-liner with great care and don't inject profane material into your speech just because it shocks; that's a desperate cop out and it doesn't impress. On the contrary, you can often earn yourself extra points for being both funny and clean at the same time.

Over the years, as a speechmeister, I've learned that a well-written humorous speech which manages to avoid vulgarity will win you respect from an audience.

This will enhance your image and up your reputation.

Nearly every client of mine has upped his reputation ...
... up yours!

BAD NEWS

The treatment of bad news in your speech should, of course, be handled with a great deal of care.

During a crisis, your audience will be wondering:

◆ What exactly has happened?
◆ How will it affect me?
◆ What's being done about it?

The use of humour is as tricky as Dicky when it comes to unpleasant tidings; it could so easily backfire if your audience feels you are being too flippant about a serious state of affairs.
My suggestion is to use humour only in order to keep the situation in perspective or as a link to other topics.

You'll find a few helpful lines under 'Bad News' in the chapter entitled 'One-Liners For Speakers' at the end of the book.

BEREAVEMENT AND ILLNESS

There's always a danger, when handling certain sensitive issues such as serious illness or recent bereavement, that your audience will become sombre and that your speech will end on a sad and awkward note.
The sudden loss of a dear one, or a well-loved associate has to be acknowledged by at least one of the speakers.

If this situation is not handled with care, the speechmaker risks 'losing' his or her audience during what would otherwise have been a sparkling, laugh-a-minute extravaganza.

It's almost enough to make you wish they hadn't passed away, isn't it?

I always place these subjects about three quarters of the way through the speech, giving the speechmaker plenty of time to ease out of the poignant atmosphere and back, gently, into the laughter.

Of course, the language you use is crucial.
Avoid words like 'dead', 'killed', 'injured', 'terminal', 'senseless', etc., and use gentler and more positive language.

Try to portray the departed with a semblance of continuity, here's an example:

> You know, it's remarkable how absence can have
> an impact of its own. When an old cherished
> friend is missing from a gathering of colleagues,
> it really is very noticeable.
> Earlier this year – sadly – we lost our Marketing
> Director, Gerry Baldwin and, although we miss
> him a lot, in a special sort of way he's still sitting
> here with us tonight, joining in with the toasts
> and laughing at the jokes.
> Such is the effect Gerry continues to have upon
> those of us who enjoyed working with him.
>
> Of course, Gerry Baldwin was also a husband
> and a father, and we're all delighted to have
> Jayne Baldwin with us tonight, looking so good
> and in such great form.

(Expect applause)

> **I must say, it's particularly gratifying that Jayne
> decided to come along and share the evening
> with us, despite the fact that she knew full well
> I'd be making a speech.**
>
> **Now that takes guts!**

The whole idea is that the lines get lighter gradually so that you don't have an unseemly leap from sadness to hilarity.

However tragic the circumstances of Gerry's death, you'll notice that, while not in any way trivialising his passing, the words are totally natural and he is treated in a straightforward manner – almost as if he were on holiday.

This way, we've shown respect and affection to our absent colleague, we've kept the audience from drifting into depression and we're ready to go straight into another series of one-liners before closing the speech.

The same technique can be used to good effect at a wedding, which – they tell me – is meant to be a happy occasion.

Let's keep it that way with a little emotional ducking and diving:

> **It takes an occasion like this, when our close
> family and our good friends are with us, to
> remind us once again of those who can't be with
> us; among them, our dear Grandma who passed
> away last year, and who really would have
> enjoyed seeing Dave getting hitched ...**

And we all remember Dave's late business
partner and best friend Sean, who we lost back
in August and is sadly missed.

Sean would have been best man today and I'm
proud to step in for him ... in a way, I feel we're
sharing the job.

In any case, Dave was my best man two years
ago so at last I can get my own back!

Treat all illnesses as transient.

This doesn't mean you should belittle other people's health
problems, but bear in mind that each sufferer handles his
or her condition differently.
Be safe. Acknowledge it, but don't dwell on it.

This sort of thing should be fine:

We're all very happy to see Brenda Maley back
with us this afternoon, looking fit as a fiddle
after her recent operation.

(Expect applause)

Brenda, we're thrilled you were able to make it
today and it's good to see that you're obviously
well on the road to recovery.

Here's a form of wording which may be suitable for those
who are absent through illness:

I'm sure you'll all be pleased to hear that both
Alf Thompson and Brian Castle have come
through their tough battles and are now well and
truly on the mend – they really don't make

streetfighters like those two any more do they?

Or, if the news isn't so bright:

> If there's one person who can weather this
> particularly nasty storm, I know it's Deborah ...
> our thoughts tonight are with her and her family
> and we all look forward to seeing her back in
> action and, as usual, taking no prisoners.

*See also 'Funerals and Wakes' in the 'One-Liners For
Speakers' chapter.*

A FEW WORDS ABOUT POLITICAL CORRECTITUDE

P.C. is the natural enemy of subtlety, humour and the
English language. If you pay too much attention to this
nonsense when writing, you'll tie yourself in knots.

You'll find yourself inserting extra words into simple text
in order not to offend. Every time the word 'he' appears, it
will have to be followed by 'and she' or 'or she', regardless
of the mess it makes of the flow. Do it when you can, of
course, but don't allow it to get in the way.

Substituting 'person' for 'woman' or 'man', does nothing
for equality or even courtesy. It serves only to diffuse the
picture of a character whose description is usually vital
when we're setting a scene.

Real women honestly don't need this patronising tosh.

They know full well that the word 'mankind' is non-
exclusive.

They realise that replacing it with 'humankind' doesn't get rid of the 'man' lurking within.

So don't bend over backwards trying to be 'gender sensitive'. Most 'persons' accept that some lines just won't work for both sexes.

When roasting colleagues or friends, don't ridicule women. Don't even think about it! Flatter them with positive humour or jokes which depict them as having the upper hand. Be extra careful about personal remarks or comments on appearance. If you ignore this warning and go ahead with risky gags about the fairer sex, don't come limping to me – I can't sew 'em back on for you!

Of course, if you *are* a woman, you are allowed to say anything you wish about men. We don't mind. It's perfectly okay. Honest.

(Er ... has she gone?)

Here are a few more P.C. idiosyncrasies you may have noticed:

◆ Freedom of Speech applies only to the Political Left – any comments from the Right are usually seen as highly offensive.

◆ Smoking is regarded as anti-social, disgusting and dangerous, unless you smoke cannabis, which doesn't count.

◆ The term 'racism' applies when criticism is directed against any culture, race or group other than the English.

By the way, I'm not being particularly brave. It's just that I confidently expect this book to be in print long after Political Correctitude has been laughed out of common usage.

CLOSING YOUR SPEECH

Remember my suggested overall strategy 'Make It Easy On Yourself'? Nowhere is this philosophy more applicable than for the conclusion of your speech.

An awful lot of rubbish is written about endings. In most cases there's really no need for anything particularly clever. Once you've said what you needed to say, you simply shove a full stop down and bugger off.

People will love you for it.

Alfred Hitchcock used to end his movies that way. In films like *The Lady Vanishes* and *North By Northwest,* once the suspense was over and the story rounded off, Hitchcock was outa there!
No epilogue, no wind-down, no big finish – one line of dialogue, a smile or an embrace. Curtain!

Too often an audience knows a speech is over before the speaker does. Don't let this happen to you.

Ten to twelve minutes of a snappy one-liner-based speech can be the equivalent of a thirty minute slow-paced talk. However brilliant your material and performance, there'll come a time when your audience has had enough. The sheer quantity of quick-fire gags becomes exhausting. The laughter starts to lose just a little of its edge and you begin to sense the first stirrings of restlessness.

You have to pick up on this before it becomes a problem. Your instinct should tell you that you've done enough.

At that point, go straight to your closing section.

Go directly.
Do not pass 'Go'.
Do not collect £200.

Mark your 'retreat' point very clearly; I always fold the top right-hand corner of the page containing the closing section, and daub it with a big red star. This ensures it's easy to find, should the audience begin to go cold.

Of course, you don't want to sound like you've made an emergency stop; far better to give the impression that you've reached a natural conclusion.
So make sure you begin the closing section with, 'Ladies and Gentlemen ... ' – you can cut smoothly to that from most lines.
Run through your main bullet points again, thank them for their hospitality and that's it.

It can sometimes be fun to end with a bit of mock philosophy, or advice:

> **Remember: drink up all your coffee – there are people in India, sleeping!**

To students or school leavers:

> **You have the whole world in your hands ... don't drop it.**

To the bridegroom:

> **To keep your marriage brimming in the everloving cup –**

whenever you're wrong, admit it ...
whenever you're right, shut up!

Or finish with a toast:

I drink to your health when I'm with you
I drink to your health when alone
I drink to your health so often
I've just about buggered my own!

The last word on concluding a speech must go to American humorist Robert Orben:

You need to end with the most effective closing a speaker could have ... your mouth.

More Closings and Toasts in the 'One-Liners For Speakers' chapter.

DIRTY ROTTEN TRICKS

It's important that when you stand up to face your audience, you'll be doing so with the strength and confidence that only a carefully written, well-prepared and thoroughly entertaining speech can give you. For this reason, I make no apologies for the length of this chapter. There's a lot *to* this writing stuff. In fact, as you can see, it's not over yet. Coming up are a few thoroughly wicked ideas, designed to help make you look like a real pro.

NOTES, SCRIPT OR MEMORY?

Many experts advise against writing your speech out in full. They feel that this method would make your performance sound false and contrived.

I happen to differ. It doesn't have to be that way at all.

Let's look at the alternatives:

CUE CARDS

To start with, I think these things are distracting and look bloody poncey.

They give the impression that you've hastily jotted down a few words on some old place-cards you found a few minutes ago in the cloak-room.

A five-minute speech could contain about fifty cues. At the normal delivery speed, your card shuffling will very rapidly begin to fascinate the audience more than whatever you're saying.

NOTES ON A SHEET OF PAPER

Not too bad a method for some speeches or presentations, but remember: the one-liner format in particular, requires precise construction. All sorts of things can go wrong if your notes don't trigger the correct phrasing or if you're not prompted to use the key words.

By the time you've made a note of all the crucial bullet points, phrased them in the correct order and included the 'magic' necessary for one-liners to work properly, it's hardly worth the bother – you might as well write it out in full.

Nevertheless, in the 'Pre-Med' chapter coming up, I've thrown in a little advice for those determined to wing the thing with notes.

No extra charge. On the house. All part of the service.

LEARN IT BY HEART?

Are you kidding me?

Unless you have a photographic memory, a wealth of experience and nerves of steel, forget it! Because chances are, you will!

Haven't you got enough to think about? Why inflict upon yourself the added terror of forgetting your words?
Believe me, when you stand up to speak, you're going to need as much confidence as you can falsify.

Instead of trying to memorise a fast-moving speech of this kind, you'd do better to utilise some of my sneakier techniques. These little tricks were designed to make the audience almost unaware that you're reading the whole thing.

What's more, they work.

So instead of sitting up night after night, attempting to learn fourteen hundred crucial words, use just a fraction of that time and effort to develop the knack of presenting your speech in a natural and relaxed manner.

Here's what I recommend, starting with:

MY FAMOUS COLOURTEXT SYSTEM

Write the speech out in *full* (one side only) on reasonably heavy paper, about 7 by 9 inches (17 by 24 cm). This size is easier to handle and looks less obvious than A4. The paper shouldn't be too flimsy because the pages need to be easy to separate as you're reading.

I find block capitals are best; they're much easier to read.

If you normally use reading glasses, you can probably make the letters large enough to manage without having to use your specs. Aim for about four or five gags or sequences per page. Large letters will prove to be a great bonus; by avoiding the necessity of picking up your glasses, putting them on, taking them off and putting them on again, you'll gain an extra hand for page-turning, cigar-smoking or brandy-drinking. At the same time, you'll draw less attention to the fact that you're actually reading from a script.

You'll also look less like an old fart.

You will have to make sure, however, that the room lighting is adequate when you make the speech. Don't worry, I'll remind you again later.

Use felt-tip pens in varying colours; for instance, one joke or small paragraph in blue, the next in green. The following line could be in black, followed by purple, and so on.

Finally, underline certain key words in red.

These could be words you need to emphasise, or merely the 'bones' of a line which could be glanced at and used as shorthand. Once you are familiar with the speech, the underlined words will often trigger your memory of the entire sequence, allowing you the luxury of spending more time looking around the audience.

Very impressive. Trust me.

There's no dishonour in having a script; TV presenters work from fully-worded autocues and cue cards. Politicians read their speeches in full from those invisible reflector things we professionals call 'invisible reflector things.'

What matters is how you use it. Hang around, I've got more tricks.

I'm sure you've seen speechmakers happily reading from typewritten or handwritten sheets of A4. Realising, quite rightly, that they need to look away from the script and make some eye contact with their audience from time to time, they look up and finish a line or two from memory as they glance around the room. Then they look down again ...

Silence ... more silence ... *excruciating* silence.

A desperate and embarrassing search has begun. The poor sap has lost his place!

'Where was I? Up the top? No, I've done that bit. Somewhere about three quarters of the way down, I think ... er ... '

Trouble is, all the words on the page look exactly the same. It's just one sheet of writing.

However, with my recommended system of using coloured text, it's much less likely that you'll lose your place.

Don't be concerned. You don't need to memorise the colour you were on before you looked away from your script; for some reason, your subconscious takes care of all that. It usually leads you back to the correct place.

Practise it; even if it doesn't work for you one hundred per cent, at least you'll be able to scan the page at a faster rate.

Remember, you only have to look at the beginning of each topic to know whether it's the right one or not, and you're not going to have that many one-liners per page.

As I said at the beginning of the section on editing, the one-liner construction makes it much easier to cut whole sections of your speech in 'real-time' if necessary.

The colourtext system makes it easier still.

> If you would rather print your speech, I suggest the following font and letter size: 'Bookman Old Style – Size 18, Upper Case'.

Magicians commonly use psychology and distraction in order to manipulate their audiences. As a speaker and a rascal, I've designed one or two similar techniques. Used properly, these sneaky ploys create the effect of almost hypnotising the audience into seeing what you want them to see, and not noticing what you don't want them to see.

See?

I've already shared a few of these crafty little dodges with you, so why stop now?

Here's a little trick to make people almost unaware that, in fact, you're reading your speech word for word:

Start off with a couple of announcements – it's perfectly natural for you to be reading these – then you can go straight into your speech, still reading, and they won't even notice.

You could, perhaps, open with some fake apologies for absence. Have a look at 'Absent Friends' in the 'One-Liners For Speakers' chapter.

Or, consider something like this:

Ladies and Gentlemen, before I start, I've been asked to make the following announcements:

We've arranged a couple of extra items for you
this evening; a little later on, Stephen Lowe of
Her Majesty's Customs and Excise is going to be
coming on to show us all how to fill in one of the
new VAT forms ...

After that, Mr Dominic Riley – a self-employed
builder – will be coming on to show us all how
to fill in ... Stephen Lowe.

I'm happy to announce that our treasurer, Frank
Stanton, is celebrating a double birthday today;
Frank is fifty ... and his hair is twenty nine!

Incidentally the Heritage Secretary has just
declared Frank Stanton's toupee a National
Wildlife Sanctuary.

One word of warning though ... don't stand too
near Frank immediately after he's been dancing
...
When he overheats, you can get high from the
glue in his wig!

Ladies and gentlemen, this evening is a very
special night for all of us ...

... and you're into the speech.

People are now quite used to seeing you glancing down at
the paper, and, as long as you bring your head up and look
around the room regularly as you speak, they won't be
conscious of you reading from a script.

By the way, during your speech, always make sure your
next page is ready for you well before you come to the end
of your current page.

It's worth practising this during your rehearsal.

THE FINE TOOTH-COMB

As Sting mentioned in his very kind foreword, I wrote my first book *How To Write A Hit Song* way back in the early sixties.

The history of that book is interesting. At the time, I had no way of foreseeing that I would turn out to be the giant of English literature I am today.

Who knew?

Having therefore been assured by the publishers that the book would be ghosted for me by an experienced journalist, I simply made a few notes, included a couple of wisecracks for the amusement of the editor and handed it in.

To my horror, when the book was published, my silly send-up text was reproduced word for word. No ghost writer had been used.

Tight bastards!

There was one sequence where I wrote: 'Once you have taped the words and music of your song, go over it with a fine tooth-comb.'

As a gag to entertain the publisher, I added: '(You can buy your Mitch Murray Fine Tooth-Comb from Feldman's Ltd, price 6/-)'.

I kid you not, hundreds of postal orders came in for 'Mitch Murray Fine Tooth-Combs'.

It's rather bizarre. Most authors complain about the torture of having their precious work altered and reshaped by publisher's editors. My complaint is that my first book wasn't.

Still, readers obviously got the gist of it and it certainly seems to have pointed one bright fourteen-year-old in the right direction. The world of music is very grateful for that.

Undaunted by my earlier experience with the astute British public, I'm going to risk using that dangerous phrase again.

Now's the time to go over your completed speech with a fine tooth comb.

Begin with this check list:

1   Does my speech have a good opening?

2   Does it have the right amount of humour for the occasion?

3   Does it have the right *style* of humour for the occasion?

4   Does it have the right style of humour for the *audience*?

5   Does the speech get my message across in a memorable way?

6   Is it the right length?

7   Where did I put it?

Once you've found it again, try a rough run-through at the correct pace.

♦ As you read, imagine the laughter and allow time for it.

♦ Put in your own light and shade: you may need to deliver some passages quite gently, at other times you'll be shouting.

♦ Make sure it all rings true.
  Are you totally comfortable with the material?
  Are you stumbling over certain words or phrases?
  If so, change them but make sure you don't kill the line.

♦ Don't over-dramatise; you're not a luvvie, you're a dude! You don't need to use Semtex to burst a balloon.

♦ Check for repetition, clichés and banalities.

I'm tempted to say 'Avoid clichés like the plague!', but that would be a cheap and facile gag and therefore perfectly suitable for this book.

The real difficulty with clichés is that, by their very nature, they have become so much a part of the language, it's easy to forget they're being used so try to be conscious of them.

Of course, to be fair on these hackneyed phrases, they wouldn't have become clichés had they not been expressive and appropriate in the first place. However, their original meanings have often become obscured and, worse – people get them wrong.

You've heard the expression: 'Laughing all the way to the bank!' Well, you shouldn't have done! The correct phrase is 'Crying all the way to the bank!' So there!

The line seems to have been invented by Liberace and used in his autobiography. He wrote: 'When the reviews are bad, I tell my staff that they can join me as I cry all the way to the bank.'

The careless repetition of words and phrases is a distraction and sounds slovenly. Needless to say, I'm not talking about the deliberate use of repetition for rhythmic effect:

> **We shall fight him by land, we shall fight him by sea, we shall fight him in the air ...**
> **(Winston Churchill)**

What I have in mind is the over-use of a favourite word or phrase – often almost meaningless – like 'basically', 'at the end of the day', 'at this point in time', 'having said that'. Granted, sometimes it's difficult to avoid repetition when you're dealing with a specialised theme or a technical subject. Often, you're stuck with jargon or acronyms. Nevertheless, try really hard to find a way of varying commonly used passages.

Please, pretty please, do it for me?
Your speech will sound all the better for it.

FINISHING TOUCHES

Take it from me, you never really finish writing your speech until you've actually performed it. Right up until then, you can expect to be making all kinds of last-minute alterations and adjustments.

I wrote earlier that you get extra points with an audience if your material is, or sounds, inventive or original.

The line between 'inspired by' and 'nicked from' is a very fine one, so if you find yourself having to steal, at least make sure you do it sensibly.
Don't just pick up any old gag; you don't know where it's been.

Don't use a joke Des O'Connor told the previous night on network television – half the country would have heard it.

If you're addressing an industry of which you have no intimate experience, be careful.

For instance, you are Guest of Honour at the Hospitality Inn Hotel Group's Annual Gala Dinner:

You say ...

> **... Earlier this evening, I was delighted to hear
> your chairman announcing last year's greatly
> improved results.
> I'd like to take this opportunity of congratulating
> you all.
> It seems like only yesterday things were so bad
> in the hotel business, chambermaids were
> stealing towels from the guests ...**

To you or I, this gag may sound quite funny, but believe me it's odds-on that every bugger in that room has heard it loads of times. Unless you're one hundred per cent sure that your gag has never been heard by those working in a certain industry, don't chance it.

The same applies to lawyer jokes when you're speaking to lawyers, estate agent jokes when you're speaking to estate agents, and policemen jokes when you have the right to remain silent.

Another audience point-earner is topicality.

On the day your speech is scheduled, is anything of note due to be taking place?

- ◆ An important football match?
- ◆ An international peace conference?
- ◆ The budget?
- ◆ The result of a major court case?
- ◆ A business merger?

Try to anticipate the probable unfolding of events and have appropriate lines ready.

Topicalising old material is all in a day's work for comedy writers. Political issues, for instance, are dead easy. The cock-ups are roughly the same – only the names and places change. The same applies to sex scandals.

Oh come on, you know *exactly* what I mean!

OTHER SPEAKERS

When you are one of several speakers, remember that you are only part of a programme. You need to take into account your position in the running order, and what other speakers are liable to say.
It's not always possible to do this, but it's certainly worth a try. Your 'ally' may well be able to help with hints about the content of the other speeches.

I was invited to make a speech at Bob Monkouse's Seventieth Birthday Party. Other speakers included Denis Norden, Jeremy Beadle, Les Dennis and Jasper Carrott. The remainder of the guest list was equally staggering: Des O'Connor, Michael Aspel, Anita Harris, Lionel Blair, Vince Hill, Ronnie Barker, David Jason; the only person I'd never heard of was *me*!

It was pretty obvious that, whereas the style of the speakers would vary considerably, all the speeches would have the same double theme: Bob's fabulous career as an entertainer, and his age.

The new wonder-drug for men – Viagra – was a hot, topical subject that week. Nothing could have been more suitable for this party; it connected perfectly with a mischievous seventy-year-old who enjoyed a good roast.

Being third on the bill, however, I decided against doing any Viagra stuff at all. I reckoned it was odds-on that the first or second speaker would do some, and I'd lose impact and momentum if I tried to follow on the same topic.

We must have all had the same idea. Everybody obviously expected everybody else to do it, and Viagra was not mentioned once; by anybody.

Pity. I'm sure it would have raised a laugh.

Audiences are not always easy to fathom. For instance, when their heads are nodding, it means one of two things: either they're in complete agreement with you and approve of what you're saying, or they're fast asleep.

Besides awards for originality, ingenuity and topicality, audiences also give prizes for early retirement. You can't really go wrong if you leave them wanting a little more.
I'm sure you'd like to share many thoughts and ideas with your audience, but you simply don't have that luxury. Any sequence which seems to go on too long, *is* going on too long.

Be ruthless. Cut it.

Nothing should be allowed to spoil the rhythm of your flow. Should you start to lose your audience, you'd have to go through the whole process of warming them up again.

Is it worth it?

Don't answer that; allow me: No!

So, as I said in Chapter One, keep it short. You earn 'nil points' for a lengthy dissertation.

It is very rare that anything good comes out of a long speech. One exception was that made by vicar, Clive Southerton, who spoke for a record *fifty hours* without taking a break in order to raise £52,000 for a hospice in Prestatyn, North Wales.

Wow! Talk about a yawn-again Christian.

Pre-Med

You now have a speech that has been well-researched, written with flair and is full of fun. Naturally, you're beginning to feel a lot more relaxed about the whole deal. The plan is coming together and you're in pretty good shape.

REHEARSAL AND PRACTICE

Before you start rehearsing your speech in earnest, check it over one more time in case you missed anything important.

Are you totally comfortable with the material?

Are you stumbling over certain words or phrases?
If so, change them, but make sure you don't kill the line.

It's important that you don't start torturing yourself with doubts and vacillation. If you go through a speech again and again and again looking for trouble, you'll always find something to question. Don't drive yourself nuts. Don't risk bottling out for nothing, trust yourself.
Your earlier instinctive reaction to your own work is often the most reliable indicator. A speech is not meant to be listened to hypercritically or analysed in minute detail; it's usually heard just once, and if you think it sounds good on first hearing, chances are it's going to work. However, if

something grates on you every time you read it, re-do that section or give it the old chopperooni.

Make an extra copy of the speech and keep it safe in a separate place. You never know what can happen: a coffee spill, a hungry dog, a little absent-mindedness ...

Rehearse standing up straight and visualising your audience. Don't bother with mirrors, they'll put you off. As long as you are aware of your deportment and read the piece as if it were the actual performance, you'll be giving the speech a valid work-out.

Do it for real. Practise it at the actual speed and at the correct level of voice projection. Rehearse as many times as you feel you need to, then leave it alone.

> You may consider audio taping your performance and listening to it later in the car, or on your Walkman.

Rehearse again shortly before you leave for the venue. Put your script in a large plain non-padded envelope, along with a couple of coloured felt tip pens and some spare paper (in case of last-minute alterations, substitutions or cuts).

WINGING IT

For those of you who insist on using notes or cards rather than a full script, here's a suggestion which could help to improve your performance and reduce the risk of forgetting anything important.

First, let me explain the background to this suggestion.
I was a lazy little bastard when I was at school. I did almost no work during the term, and consequently found myself in a bit of a spot when it came to the approaching

'O' level exams.
This was a shame because I had particularly wanted to pass History.

God knows why.

Anyway, two days before the examinations, I locked myself away in the public library, divided the history syllabus into date and subject segments, and read all the various published accounts of these events.
Having done that, I composed my own composite version of each segment, based on what I had read in all those books.

This proved to be a great way of retaining knowledge.

I retained it for precisely two days, passed the exam and then forgot the lot for ever.

So if you definitely want to wing it from rough headlines, jot down three or four different versions of each segment – bearing in mind the sensitivity of any one-liners involved – and go through them a few times before settling on the final shorthand for your notes.

Hopefully, they'll stick in your memory well enough to do the job.

I'm still not sure why you want to do it the hard way though. You can make a full script sound just as natural if you write it properly and read it well.

VISUALS

I *hate* visuals. Hate 'em, hate 'em, hate 'em!

They get in the way and very rarely help.
Too often, they merely mirror the supporting documents

every member of the audience is already holding.
Too often, they stop the audience thinking.

Unfortunately, sometimes they really are necessary for graphic depictions, so make sure you rehearse the technical stuff with the same care you take over the words.

Learn to operate whatever it is you wish to operate as smoothly as you can.

Don't stop speaking, press a button then continue. It should be a smooth, seamless action.
If anything, the image should be up there slightly ahead of you.

It's always a good idea to give yourself a reminder a few seconds before its time, in order for you to anticipate the next slide or other device.
On your script, in the preceding paragraph or segment, draw a purple star, or an orange circle or some other shape in the margin.
That way, you won't suddenly arrive at the cue point and lose impact by starting the process at such a late stage.

Rehearse reading, speaking and clicking until the whole operation is silky smooth.

If someone else is operating the visual aid, either give them a copy of the cued-up script and rehearse until you get nosebleed, or devise a subtle signal system and train the operator to perform as if he or she were a musician.

Smooth, smooth, smooth.

ON THE DAY OF THE SPEECH

Remember what I wrote earlier about the extra points you earn for being topical? Well buster, today's the day.

Now's the time to insert any last-minute material into your speech.

What's the big talking point in the papers this morning?

How's the weather? Is it remarkable enough for comment?

Have there been any last minute developments connected with the topic of your speech or the characters mentioned in it?

Late-breaking issues are usually best handled by the device of an announcement at the very beginning. It's a good idea to take your audience reward-points early if you can. The crowd gets a warm-up, and you get a nice boost for your confidence.

Again, don't contrive. We come back to this 'truth' thing. If it's a quiet news day and there's nothing to say, don't say anything. You either need an important story you can work with, or a real comedy opportunity you can't resist.

Before you start adding new material, give your 'ally' a ring to check on any last-minute changes, such as absentees or extra guests. These late circumstances will also have to be accounted for in your script.
While you're on the line, check that someone will be introducing you, and that they know what to say about you. If necessary, write something and fax it to them.

Rehearse your speech another three or four times, but stop

before you go stale. By now, everything should be cool, so allow your mind to clear a little. The material needs to sound fresh to *you* as well.

You'll need to get to the venue rather early. You have quite a few things to do there before the evening gets under way. Don't forget to take your little Junior Speechmaker's Kit. Namely, the large, plain non-padded envelope, a couple of coloured felt tip pens, some spare paper and a handkerchief for mopping your brow.

Once there, find a friendly banqueting manager, head waiter or whoever else is responsible for the function, introduce yourself and ask if you could see the room in which you'll be speaking.

People are usually very helpful to speakers in much the same way as a prison warder is considerate towards the poor guy about to be executed. They're just delighted it's not them.

Check out the room:

♦ Will everyone be able to see you?

> Your speaking position is very important. I personally like to speak with my back to the wall and an audience equally divided left and right in front of me.
> I also much prefer to speak from the top table or from within the crowd rather than having to perform from the stage, unless I'm there as a platform guest. The stage becomes a barrier between you and the audience and interferes with that special intimate relationship. Instead of speaking as part of the crowd, the platform or dance floor makes it a case of 'us and them' and you may not get the results your material deserves.
> If you're a little nervous, it's rather comforting to be close to other people, especially folk with whom you've

developed a mini relationship over dinner.

How sweet.

Of course, it isn't always possible to make your speech under ideal conditions. Believe me, there are some very weird-shaped rooms around, and quite often half the crowd can't see a bloody thing whatever the set-up.
Why anyone should actually choose these mini-mazes for their evenings, I've no idea. Still, sometimes that's what you have to work with, so try to position yourself as best you can.
If you need to change your speaking location from the one allocated to you, the banqueting manager probably won't be able to help. You'll have to find your 'ally' or one of the organisers in order to get the change authorised.

◆ Will you be able to see your script?

Check out the lighting. Don't be fooled by the brightness of the room at this stage; banqueting staff usually make their preparations with the lights full on. Once the guests arrive, these are dimmed for purposes of atmosphere, and you could find yourself really struggling to read your script at speech time. Work out the correct lighting level for your requirements, and arrange for someone reliable to operate them at the appropriate time.

◆ Will everybody be able to hear you?

You'll be reading from a full script, so you'll need both hands available throughout your speech.
One hand will be holding the paper, the other will need to be free for page-turning, elaborate gestures, slide operation, water-sipping, pill-popping, toasting or – should you insult the wrong guy – self defence.

It's almost essential, therefore, to ensure that you have a free-standing microphone.

I prefer a table stand, but any mike stand will do. It's a good idea to arrange for this in advance, but don't put too much trust in people who tell you to leave it all to them; it's your responsibility, you're the one who'll look awkward if things are not right. Some of these helpful individuals turn out not to be around at the crucial time for one reason or another, or they forget, or they don't speak English well enough to know what you're talking about.

Personally, I take no chances. I have my *own* microphone stand, and – where necessary – I schlep it along with me.

By the way, it's a good idea to tip your friendly assistant quite handsomely. Sometimes this can do real wonders. As if by magic, they can find things they don't have, fix things that can't be mended and bring you free drinks all through the evening.

Most sound systems are fiestas of feedback. Your voice projection will vary considerably during a spirited performance, so take this early opportunity of testing the amplification set-up by saying a few words at various volume levels.

At no stage – now or later – should you test the mike by blowing on it or saying, 'One two, one two!'. If you do, I'll come over there and knock your bloody block off myself! Right?

◆ Finally, check out any other accessories – projectors, video, monitors – you will be using.

PUNTER POSITIONING

Here's another of those dirty rotten tricks. (Don'tcha love 'em?)

Ask your 'ally' to show you the table plan, or at least to point out where each of the characters you'll be featuring is seated. Where their segment or mention appears on the script, draw a little arrow pointing towards his or her seating position. This enables you to direct your comments accurately towards the subject of your gag.

Brilliant, eh?

Well, that's what I'm paid for.

HIDE YOUR SPEECH

Once you've completed all these little tasks, put your speech back in its envelope, and slide it between the table and tablecloth at your place setting. (Now you know why it has to be a flat envelope, not a padded one.)

You are now ready to start drinking and mingling.

I called this chapter 'Pre-Med' because it parallels the necessary preparation work carried out before a medical procedure.

We've checked out the equivalent of the operating theatre, we've readied our assistants, we've prepared our instruments.

It's now time for the anaesthetic.

I'm a brandy man. What's yours?

This is it – Fright Night!

Aren't you pleased you got there early? Apart from the important tasks you had to attend to, you've been spared the extra psychological terror of walking into a crowded room and being thoroughly overwhelmed. This way, as one of the first people there, the crowd is building up around you, gradually. You have time to meet more of them, to socialise, to fraternise, to *brandyise*.

Try to meet as many of the characters featured in your speech as possible, particularly the ones you don't know very well.
Once you've met them and talked to them, you'll be seen as having more right to roast them.
Learn a little more about these people. It may well have a positive subliminal effect upon the way you put the lines across. It's also a final opportunity to make any cuts should you realise you've misrepresented anyone.

Ask if they have any objection to being 'sent up' and promise them you won't be vicious.
(If someone says 'Yes, I object.', do it anyway. A pompous son of a bitch like that deserves even less mercy than a good sport.)

Don't quote or discuss any of the lines from your forthcoming speech, you'll spoil the whole effect. Protect that element of surprise.

Get as friendly as you can with everyone you meet, even the utter prats. It's worth it for the wonderful warm feeling you get from an audience packed with supporters.

FACING FOOD

Don't be concerned if you find you've lost your appetite; this is a common symptom of pre-speech collywobbles. After the speech you'll be starving and all the food will be gone, so think ahead; when they start serving, slip the waiter a fiver, and ask him to keep something for you.

CLEVER WAYS WITH BOOZE

While you're waiting to speak, level with yourself:

Are you slurring words?

Are you liable to sway? or see double? or burp? or worse?

If the answer to any of these questions is 'yeshh', don't be too alarmed; at least you've proved that the alcohol is working properly.

However, as a speechmaker, you have a problem.

You must switch immediately to water.

I know, I know, it's horrible stuff, and yes I do realise what fishes do in it, but you've swallowed too much poison and water is the antidote.

Drink as much water as you can, as fast as you can – whether you feel like it or not.
Inevitably you'll suddenly find yourself doing a lot of

travelling, but that's just nature's way of helping the water to circulate around your system. You should be straightened out within ten to fifteen minutes, but keep that water handy; you'll need it during your speech, and here's why:

Nerves have a really interesting effect upon an inexperienced speaker. Your mouth suddenly dries up. It feels like someone has stuffed a ball of blotting paper into it. As you try to speak, your tongue sticks to the roof of your mouth and you suddenly wish you had Teflon gums!

It's a most peculiar phenomenon and one which requires a good supply of H_2O most of the way through your speech.

But let's turn this into an advantage:

Plan on using the glass of water as a prop. It can have the same effect as George Burns' cigar: a punctuation device assisting in the control of your audience.

After you hit 'em with a one-liner, take a drink while they're laughing. In a short while, you'll find the crowd will begin to co-operate with you by stretching out their laughs until you've finished drinking.

This is another example of audience hypnosis. You are giving them subtle signals. You're almost ordering them to laugh and then rest on command.

> Don't forget, once your speech is over, go straight back to alcohol; after all, you don't want to make a habit of this water thing, do you? Just think: if water can rot the soles of your shoes, imagine what it can do to your stomach!

FRESHENING UP

About half an hour before you are due to speak, go to an appropriate room and freshen up.

Splash water on your face, brush your teeth, take a few deep breaths, yawn to loosen your throat, stretch your limbs.
That's much better, isn't it?

Now, return to your table and quietly remove your script from its hiding place. If you get an opportunity, have a secret last-minute glance at the first couple of lines, then sit on it.

Quite literally.

Make sure your glass (your 'prop', remember?) is loaded up with water, then make animated conversation until the chairman bangs his gavel. Doing this is a whole lot better than just sitting there allowing extra tension to build up for no good reason.

Bang! Bang! Bang!

The moment has arrived. You're about to be introduced. Most of your fears should, by this time, have been neutralised. Any residual anxiety is almost certainly that healthy adrenaline-charged anticipation I wrote about earlier. You'll probably feel it as a little buzz between the solar plexus and the throat.

This is good. It shows that you're taking the assignment seriously. It shows you care.
Be quietly proud of those nerves, but don't dump them on your audience. They might not be subtle enough to buy all

that crap I just tried to reassure you with.

Seriously, you're armed with a great speech, you're fresh, you're alert and you're more than ready to get on with it.

I was once booked to make a speech at a small literary lunch. Predictably, I found myself eating really lousy food and surrounded by a very dreary crowd.
As I sipped my lukewarm over-brewed coffee, waiting to be introduced, an elderly gentleman sitting at my table leaned towards me and said, 'I suppose you're ready and really eager to go.'
'Yes', I said, 'But I've got to make this speech first.'

WHISTLE A HAPPY TUNE

The old song has the answer: whenever you feel nervous, hold your head up high and project the bare-faced lie that you have all the confidence in the world.

(The song lyric says it better, but I'm not allowed to mention the word 'erect'.)

A lot depends on the first few seconds immediately after you've been introduced. The way you stand up, walk across (if you need to), and take the microphone.
You must never allow your audience to feel nervous on your behalf. *Their performance is nearly as important as yours.*

You'll be relying on their infectious reactions to inspire each other and to encourage you, so it really helps if they immediately sense your confidence. (Even if it's not the real thing.)
Don't forget, they're on your side. They're all charged up, ready to have fun. It's in their interest to support you.

Your *bearing* is part of it. Make yourself as tall as you can. Look around at your audience.
Smile. Not a nervous smile, a nice strong smile.
Strength is part of what you need to project.

The mere fact that you're doing what most people dread empowers you in their eyes. They're impressed and slightly intimidated by you, even at this stage.

(Little do they know, eh?)

Take your time. Make 'em wait just a little.

Establishing your authority in this way gains respect and begins the process of training your audience.

When you speak, speak strongly, speak clearly and speak with self-assurance. After all, you can afford to be bold when your material is strong. And of course, it is.

DISGUISING THE SHAKES

You'll be holding your script in one hand, and you'll be using the other hand for page-turning, drinking and pointing to people as their names come up. If you are using a rostrum, you'll have both hands free at times.

Many speakers worry about what they should do with their hands. After hearing some of them, I'm tempted to suggest they try putting them over their mouths. Not very constructive I know, but I'm like that.

What happens with your hands becomes a highly important issue if you happen to be a trembler.

Trembling is a very strange phenomenon. It's pretty

common to be speaking or performing quite happily with absolutely no feeling of nervousness, only to find you've been shaking like mad.

Something to do with the subconscious, I suppose. Who knows?

One thing's for sure: trembling is far more noticeable to you than it is to your audience.
Nevertheless, let's try to disguise it as best we can.

◆ First of all, refuse to acknowledge it. It has nothing to do with you. Concentrate harder on the speech.

◆ If, despite this denial, you find your script is shaking too much, move it around. Use it as part of your posturing. Glance at the next couple of lines and do them off the cuff while anchoring your script to your hip or dropping it to your side. The secret is to keep it on the move.

◆ If your free hand is trembling, shove it in your side pocket, or transfer the script from your other hand, or jab it in the air if appropriate to the text.

◆ Don't hold on to your drinking glass longer than the time needed to drink from it. Combining water with the shakes is just plain dumb. And very carbonating.

> To keep things running smoothly and to avoid gaps in your delivery, always make sure your next page is ready for you well before you come to the end of your current page.
>
> Keep your thumb under the page you're reading from, and use it to lift the paper as soon as you get to the last line.

THE LANGUAGE OF LAUGHTER

It's funny how a laugh can say so much more than just 'Ha Ha'.

When you really listen to audience laughter, you begin to realise that each episode defines its own reaction to the joke that induced it.
The tone, pitch and length of a laugh is like its DNA.
Every chuckle, every giggle, every shriek of hilarity carries with it, it's own unique message.

One laugh can say:

◆ 'I've heard that one before, but it's good to hear it again.'

Another laugh can say:

◆ 'What a clever line. Thanks for the work you put into it.'

A laugh can say:

◆ 'Oops, that's naughty!'

It can say:

◆ 'Get on with it for Gawd's sake!'

It can say:

◆ 'We all saw that one coming.'

It can say:

◆ 'Wow! I didn't expect that!'

It can say:

◆ 'Yes, I know exactly what you mean.'

The laugh you want to hear at the very beginning of your speech is one that says: 'What a great start. You're obviously going to be very funny.'
This is the ideal psychological boost for the terrified speaker, and is almost guaranteed to nuke anyone's nervousness. However, don't let it throw you if you don't immediately get the laugh you were hoping for. Your audience will often be slower to react at the beginning of your piece than at the end.

Although you may know each one of them really well as individuals, together they have become an audience and you have become a speaker. As such you're new to each other.

You need to re-assess your relationship.

These individuals have now adopted a collective essence. They have become a separate creature and will react in an organic way.

It sounds like a load of crap, doesn't it? But it really is true.

You now need to learn about the way they react as an audience, and they – in turn – need to get the hang of you as a speechmaker.
They need to tune in to your material and to the way you deliver it. This can sometimes take a little time, but we're only talking minutes.

They'll soon warm up. Honest.

DHL – Delivery of Hot Lines

Making a speech for the first time is very much like making love for the first time.
Because you may not have total confidence in what you're doing, the temptation is to rush it.

She's going to change her mind, I'm going to lose it, we're going to be interrupted – oh.

At first, you may be unsure as to how well your speech is going to be received:

Is the material funny enough?
Is that one-liner in poor taste?
Am I trying too hard?

Rushing into the next line too early is a sure sign that you are losing your nerve. Control it. If you've been following my advice, your material is great. Stay cool.

Of course you have doubts – that's why you've been reading *Mitch Murray's Handbook For The Terrified Speaker* – but you're committed now, and you mustn't be tempted to garble your talk.

Speak slower and louder than you would in everyday conversation. As you deliver a line, wait just a little before you jump in with the next. As I illustrated earlier, sometimes a gag will produce a delayed reaction and by the time the laughter builds up to its peak, you're halfway through the next line if you're not careful.
So let the laughter run its course, and when it's just beginning to taper off, come in strong with the next gag.

You have to be sensible about this of course. Don't stand

up there in total silence; if a joke dies, bury it swiftly by delivering the next.

You'll often find that a few sharp members of the audience will pick up on a line, whereas others will miss it.

Help them out – pause. Smile at the clever ones who caught on. Give the slower members of the audience a little time to get the message signalled to them by the sharper ones. The early laugh forces the slower elements in the crowd to think about the gag in order to see why it was funny.

The result of this is that the joke ends up sounding clever rather than the audience sounding stupid.

You can't lose either way.

As you speak, gaining strength and confidence from every incoming laugh, vary your vocal pitch, put some music into your intonation, inject light and shade into your performance.

A few pages back, I wrote this about audiences: *'Their performance is nearly as important as yours.'*

It's quite remarkable how encouraging the response of an audience can be to a speaker.
I once saw Senator Ted Kennedy – the 1969 Chappaquidick Free-Fall Driving Champion – make a speech at a small dinner in Washington. The subject was the importance of copyright protection and Kennedy was reading from notes.

The beginning of his speech was rambling and unimpressive. He spoke in very general terms and seemed to lack conviction. Gradually though, he started getting louder and sounding more confident. He was noticeably feeding off the growing response of the audience.

Suddenly, he dispensed with the notes and began to give a staggering demonstration of expert oratory, culminating in a breathtaking climax.

My colleague Peter Callander and I leapt to our feet along with everyone else, and wholeheartedly applauded Kennedy's remarkable performance. As we clapped, we reeled at what we were doing. Peter said, 'Would you ever have believed that you and I would be standing up to applaud this guy?'

'Never'.

Up until then, Peter and I had regarded Ted Kennedy as seedy and anti-British. Although his performance didn't change our opinion of the man, it deserved recognition and respect. That day, Kennedy showed us something of the magic of his clan, and demonstrated why millions of Americans took him seriously.
Some guys have it, some guys don't.

There's no doubt about it, audiences collaborate with good speakers. The power generated by a positive reaction is amplified and bounced back. As the audience becomes more excited, so does the speaker. Adolf Hitler was reputed to become sexually aroused to the point of ejaculation by the way crowds at Nuremberg responded to his impassioned speeches.
Charlie Chaplin parodied this effect in *The Great Dictator*, where Hinkel (Chaplin) works himself into a frenzy during a speech and, eventually, has to throw a glass of water down the inside of his trousers.

By the way, don't try this trick at home. All you'll get is a cheap laugh and wet pants.

Think your way through your performance. Be totally aware of what you're saying.

Be like a good actor. Believe it.
Even if you're tossing out an outrageous insult, believe it!

Remember, you happen to be talking to *people* not walls and ceilings. Don't be shy about looking directly at your audience.

I like to talk to clusters of three or four at a time, but I avoid fixing on any one person unless he or she is laughing too loud, heckling or coughing – in which case, naturally, I try to have a little fun with them.

Some experts recommend that you start a sentence by looking at one group of people, and end it by turning to another. I think that's a pretty good idea – it certainly adds a little animation to your performance – but it can look a little contrived if you do too much of it.

There's no need to be coy about laughing at your own jokes occasionally; it's quite endearing and further bonds you with your audience. You're making them feel like they're part of the action. In a way, you're saying, 'What a daft gag, let's enjoy it together.'

Giggling at what you just said yourself can also be useful as a timing prop. Like drinking water, it's something to do while you wait for your laugh, or turn your page. The difference is, however, you can't do too much of it, and you can't do it for too long.

If you find that your mouth is drying up, don't leave it until it becomes a real problem, deliver your next funny line and, during the laugh, take a sip. They'll wait. In fact, as I said before, they'll stretch out the laugh to give you enough time.

If you need a drink during a serious section, you'll have to *induce* a helpful giggle by preceding your first gulp with,

'As you can see, this is a powdered speech ... you have to add water.', or, 'Oh yes, that reminds me, this speech is sponsored by Beefeaters.'

WORKING THE ROOM

Nothing is one hundred per cent reliable when it comes to speaking in public. That's what makes the whole business so exciting and, at the same time, utterly nerve-racking.
A gag which usually inspires loud guffaws, could one day – for no apparent reason – die the death of a thousand cuts. Conversely, a pretty ordinary one-liner might suddenly spark off an epidemic of hilarity so severe, they'd have to call in the paramedics.

Go figure.

If you were to handpick sixty people to be your audience every time you made a speech, they would still react quite differently each time they were assembled.
All you can do is play the numbers game. Choose the best material you can for the right size and type of audience, and you'll score with it nearly every time. However, if a certain gag is destined to fail that day, it'll bomb whether your audience is nine people or nine hundred. The laws of probability don't apply to audience size.

When speaking to a very small audience, your style should be intimate and easy-going, your gestures modest, your performance subtle.

If you're in a large room – a conference centre for instance – you need to be more elaborate, the expressions you use should be bigger, your language should be a tad less casual.

You'll also find that in a big venue, for some strange reason, the laughter will radiate away from you in waves. People in the first few rows will seem to react to your gags well before those at the back.

I can't explain this phenomenon. I can only assure you that the effect has nothing to do with the speed of sound.
So be even more careful with your pace and learn to allow for this bizarre delay.

Be prepared for an occasional burst of applause.

It's a great compliment.

The audience are telling you they think you're clever and they're grateful you took the trouble to offer them such a good line. Spontaneous applause usually happens when a joke is 'right on the button', or if you've come up with a timely topical gag, or if you've zapped out an effective ad lib or unrehearsed reaction.

Be proud, you've just been awarded audience points.

EXPECTING THE UNEXPECTED

I want you to be brave about what I'm going to tell you now.

You're going to make mistakes. Quite a few of them.
Some of them will be noticeable, some won't.

Every speaker makes mistakes, there are no exceptions. Experienced speakers, however, are able to walk straight through them, or shrug them off with a clever line or a giggle. They refuse to be thrown, and so should you.

Accept these human errors. Don't draw attention to them if they're not particularly obvious. Even if the audience notices the slip-up, it's soon forgotten.

If you happen to leave out a one-liner, or even a complete section of your speech, don't go back. This can be fatal. Firstly, it involves you in two searches:

1   Tracking down the missing sequence.

2   Trying to find your way back to where you were.

Secondly, although many of these lines and sequences are independent segments, they are not necessarily 'stand-alone' in the context of your speech. In the excitement of your real-time emergency, you'll never remember how much any particular line relies on the one which precedes it or on the one which follows it.

It's history. Leave it and move on.

Be cool about your mistakes, but equally avoid over-reacting to a great response. A sudden ovation is very flattering and is bound to be well deserved, but you must accept it as quietly and naturally as you can – as if you expected it.

Don't be arrogant, and don't be tempted to start showing off by attempting to do things you haven't prepared. Professionals don't 'wing it'. They might *look* as if they do, but usually everything is carefully worked out.

There are always going to be intangibles of course: sudden noises, strange audience behaviour, interruptions, technical problems.

These things happen and, by their very nature, it's impossible to be ready for every circumstance.

Some of these occurrences are provided for with verbal remedies in the 'One-Liners For Speakers' chapter under categories such as 'Smart-Arse Quips', 'Heckle Lines' and 'Savers and Ad Libs'.

Hey! Wouldn't it be lovely if you could memorise the lot, drawing on just the right line at just the right time?

Yeah, right.

The good news is that some incidents are very common, and you can make arrangements to sound as if you're reacting brilliantly to an unexpected moment.

For instance, someone invariably forgets to go to the toilet before the speeches. As they try to creep out unnoticed, you say:

Excuse me, if you're going for a pizza, could you bring me back a tomato and pepperoni please?

A heckler shouts out something unintelligible.
You say: **I'll name that tune in one.**

Someone's beeper or pager goes off.
You say: **Sir ... your chicken's cooked!**

If you're faced with lots of noise from a section of the audience while you're trying to speak, don't react by getting louder. On the contrary, speak softer. This way, there's a good chance that other members of the audience will shut them up for you. Most people will want to hear what you have to say and, nine times out of ten, the situation will be sorted.
Whatever happens, don't lose your cool. Keep your dignity intact and, if necessary as a last resort, go straight to your ending and sit down. In other words, quit while you're behind.

No one will blame you, but there may well be a few bodies in the car park a little later.

Have a few pseudo ad libs written at the top of each page of your script. You may include one or two heckle-management comments, or an aside, or a 'saver' for no laughs.
The same lines should be repeated on every page. After all, you never know when you'll be needing them and you certainly won't have time to go looking. Make sure they're right there in front of you at all times.

Joey Bishop – the night club comic – was right in the middle of his Las Vegas act when the fabulous Marilyn Monroe, looking as stunning as ever and tracked by two spotlights, swept into the room along with her entourage.
Every head turned, following this exquisite creature as she made her way to her table.
Far from being overawed by her presence, Bishop came up with one of the greatest ad lib lines of all time: 'Hey! I thought I told you to wait in the truck!'

TIME TO GO

And now, a few words – *not* from the Governor of The Bank of England, but from our old friend, humorist Robert Orben:

> **The Interest Rate is coming down**
> **Of this there is no doubt**
> **You know it when your audience**
> **Is slowly walking out.**

Remember my advice about closing your speech early if necessary?

Ideally, of course, you won't have this problem. Your talk will be the right length, and you'll sail through it, leaving them wanting more. However, should your instinct begin to tell you their listening is lessening, it's time to break for the border, amigo.

Think of it from the audience's point of view; they're still enjoying the speech and the jokes, but the little stings and surprises are no longer unexpected. Although they don't know the nature of the surprise, they're now conditioned to *expect* a surprise. Subliminally, they have had just the right amount of you. The fading edge of their reactions is telling you this.

Don't be precipitous. Don't look for it. Let them tell you in their own subtle way. Make sure in your own mind that you've reached the peak of your welcome, then it's 'Hasta la vista baby! I'll be back.' When they hear you signing off, they'll feel a tinge of regret that it's all over, but they'll be comfortably satisfied.

I know I've paid quite a bit of attention to this subject of 'premature evacuation', so let me reassure you that most speeches actually last the distance. It's not all that often you need to cut and run, but at least now you know how to do it.

Well, here we are at the end of the speech.
Relieved? Of course you are.
However, it's also the end of your very special and magical relationship with the audience, and that's a little sad.

Never mind; you've danced to the sweet music of laughter, revelled in the sublime thrill of spontaneous applause and are about to wallow in the ecstasy of adulation.

Well done. Enjoy it. You've earned it!

Post-Op

We come now to the process of winding-down, during which you'll experience a vast range of feelings – some justified, some irrational. You may feel elated or self-critical, you may feel relieved or concerned, you may feel a sense of accomplishment, or you could feel very empty.

These feelings are only partly connected with your actual performance. They're the normal symptoms of an anti-climax. After all, you've worked on this project for a long time. It's become part of your life. There were moments when you were in love with it, there were moments when you hated its guts. It's haunted you, it's absorbed you, it's stimulated you, it's motivated you, and suddenly, in the space of just a few minutes – it's all over.

The best thing you can do at this stage is to start paying some serious attention to that brandy. You don't want too much blood getting into your alcohol stream, do you?

Save the de-briefing for later. You continue to be on show. People are still watching you and you really ought to look as if you've taken everything in your stride. If another speaker is about to stand up, you'll have to pretend to concentrate – in much the same way as they pretended to concentrate on *your* speech.

Don't forget to put your script back into its envelope and sit on it again. If you leave it lying around, you might forget to take it home with you. Worse: someone may get curious and discover all those clever tricks and secrets. Who's going to buy my book when they can get all that information from something you've carelessly discarded? How could you do this to me after all I've done for you? I've got a family, I've got children, I've got expensive girlfriends, I've got an overdraft, I've got … completely off the subject.

Where was I?

Oh yes, I want to tell you about compliments.

You may not have realised this, but there's a bit of a knack to being able to accept compliments gracefully. If your speech was as good as it should have been, I have a feeling that a few hints in this area may be useful to you.

Firstly, don't contradict a compliment. You may think saying something like, 'Oh no, I was really off-form tonight' sounds nice and modest, but it's really a slap in the face for someone who has actually taken the trouble to let you know how much they enjoyed listening to you.

On the other hand, you can't say, 'Yes, bloody great wasn't I?'

The safest response is to thank them for being so thoughtful and tell them how grateful you are for the valuable feedback. Listen to what they have to say. You can nearly always learn something worthwhile from a customer.

Some compliments may go slightly over the top. After a few drinks and an enjoyable time, someone could feel compelled to come up to you and say, 'That was the best speech I've ever heard in my entire life. You're a genius!'

This is a little bit like a girl saying, 'You're the best lover I've ever had'. She may well believe it at the time, but there's no reason why *you* should. Be gracious and modest as you receive this accolade, but remember, it's always wiser – for the sake of your own balance – to assume she's only getting a bit carried away. So it is with speechmaking; you can't afford to be complacent. Every time you stand up to speak you're faced with a brand new challenge. Every time is different.

If you're at all like me, you won't be able to avoid agonising over the speech you just made. For quite a long time, you'll find yourself reviewing the things you should have said but didn't, the things you shouldn't have said but did.

You'll be puzzled at why the reaction to some pretty ordinary throw-away lines was suprisingly good, and you'll be trying to analyse why the audience was totally indifferent to one or two of your best jokes.

The audience, like the customer, is always right. They prescribe the benchmark. You have to work to their rules. It's no use saying, 'The speech was a great success, but the audience were miserable failures'.

See it their way. Learn from it. Deal with it.

> If public speaking is liable to become a regular thing for you, try to record your performance every now and then. You'll be able to monitor your diction, the way you deliver your lines, timing, gags that go well, gags that die a death, delayed-reaction gags ...
>
> Making a speech is such a highly-charged event that it's difficult to remember details like these once it's over. Try listening to a replay. You'll learn so much, and it'll help make the next speech even better.

So, my little terrified speaker, how are you feeling now?

A little easier, I'm sure.

You probably assumed that reading this book has kept you so busy, you haven't had time to be nervous.

Wrong.

Remember what I said in the introduction about how we were going to address each of your individual fears and break them down into manageable segments? Remember how I promised that as you began to learn how to handle each of these concerns, your overall anxiety would start to dissipate?

Well, that's what's been happening and, trust me, it'll continue.

Of course you're always going to have a few nervous moments, it would be most unhealthy if you didn't, but you have my word of honour as a gentleman and a poker player that your entire career as a terrified speaker can now be summed up in one word: over!

One-Liners for Speakers

This is not primarily a book of one-liners, so the small selection I have put together has been designed to help you find and utilise quips, zingers and bits of business not normally found in other joke books.

There are, of course, some general roast lines and character insults – I'm only human after all – but I've concentrated on material likely to be useful when interacting with an audience.

> The names of characters featured in the following one-liners are for the purpose of illustration only. Any resemblance they may have to certain prats you know personally, is purely a stroke of luck.

ABSENT FRIENDS

Richard Thompson can't be with us this evening, he's going into hospital. Apparently, surgeons have finally come up with a great idea designed to help with his drinking problem ... they're going to open him up and Scotchguard his liver!

(Bridging line)

Duncan Bradley can't be with us tonight; he's
had to satisfy demands from abroad ...
This time, the broad is a Mrs Doris Appleyard
from Leicester.

(Bridging line)

Alex Taylor apologises, he can't be with us this
evening.
Domestic problems, I'm afraid.
A few weeks ago, he and his wife bought a
water-bed and ever since then, they've been
slowly drifting apart.

(Bridging line)

John Perry couldn't make it this evening.
Hey, do you realise what that means? Prayer
really does work.

Tonight, ladies and gentlemen, our Vice-
President David Swannage has honoured
us with his absence!

Actually, I treasure every moment I don't see
him.

Doug Fletcher was due to be here this evening,
but I have to inform you that he wasn't able to
come ...
I *have* to inform you of that because otherwise,
believe me, you'd never have noticed.

(Bridging line)

Jack Peters can't be here and I must say I miss him.
I always miss Jack – I'm a rotten shot!

Our special guest this evening needs no introduction whatsoever ... he didn't show up!

Stan Pearce apologises, he can't be with us tonight ... no one invited him.

Harry Fisher won't be coming along this evening; he couldn't make bail.

(Bridging line)

Noel Phillips couldn't make it tonight – but then, according to Elaine, he couldn't make it last night either ... or the night before ... or the night before that.

(Bridging line)

Finally, Mike Bennett apologises, he can't be here; it's the baby's night off and he's got to look after the baby-sitter.

ADVICE

The easiest way to stay awake during an after-dinner speech is to be the one giving it.

If you can tell the difference between good advice and bad advice, you don't need advice.

Never buy a genuine Van Gogh from a guy in a Bond Mini Van.

How do you ensure success in the equity markets?
According to the late Will Rogers, it's simple:
'Buy some good stock. Hold it till it goes up ... and then sell it.
If it doesn't go up, don't buy it!'

As you get older, you become wiser, so get married while you're still stupid.

Love is forever ... pack your bags accordingly.

Tips for first-time parents, No.34: All new-born babies are wrinkled; do *not* try to iron them!

Ladies, if your husband chases anything in skirts, cure him by taking him to the Highland Games this year.

The old theory was: marry an older man because they're more mature. But the new theory is: men don't mature, marry a younger one.
(Rita Rudner)

Hug and squeeze and kiss her daily ... and if her daily won't go along with it, try the au pair!

Don't be sexist. Birds hate that.

Never turn your back on anything that can bleed
for five days and still live!

I'd like to end my speech with a piece of advice ...
Never end a speech with a piece of advice.

ANNOUNCEMENTS

I'm happy to announce that your generosity in
buying tickets and attending tonight's event, also
indirectly benefits local children here in the
Central Manchester area ...
Yes, even as we speak the little bastards are in
the car park, going through your cars!

I've had a message for Bob Prentice from the East
Wimbledon Sperm Bank: Bob, could you please
give them a ring first thing in the morning ...
your sperm bounced!

I'm happy to announce that first prize in the
Ralph Collier Lookalike Contest is a gift voucher
for the plastic surgeon of your choice!

(Bridging line)

For reasons of safety, the organisers have
requested that at the end of this talk, you refrain
from getting up on to the tables or chairs during
my standing ovation.

I have the honour to announce that Lionel Morris
has just been awarded the Freedom of the City!
(Encourage applause)
In case you'd like to be there to support him, the
presentation will be taking place next week in
the city itself ... Sarajevo.

Will the owner of toupee, serial number 73417,
kindly collect it from the foyer ... it's beginning
to confuse the cat.

BAD NEWS

Well, it's been a 'garden hose up the exhaust
pipe' kinda year.

I'd like to say that next year looks like being our
best ever ...
Boy, would I like to say that!

The good news is that we have almost everything
we need.
The bad news ... none of it is paid for!
(Bridging line)

I'd rather not go into that; it's so sad, I might cry
and dilute my brandy!
(Bridging line)

They say that misery loves company, but lately it seems to love *this* company.

It's easy to say business is improving ...
Saying it with a straight face is the problem.

I have good news and bad news. First, the good news:
Ian Parkin is going to sing for us all this evening ... and that'll give you some idea of how bad the bad news is!

I'll never forget the time a man knocked on my door in the middle of the night and said, 'I have some good news and some bad news. First the good news: You have the right to remain silent ...'

I don't really want to comment on the latest figures, but I think I should take this opportunity of announcing our proposed new logo: it's a picture of a canoe without a paddle!

I've just had some good news and some bad news about my daughter's driving test.
The good news? She got eighteen out of twenty!
The bad news? We're talking pedestrians here!

Here's more bad news ... that was my best joke!

CLOSINGS

Finally ... I bet *that's* a word you're happy to hear ...

Thank you for listening. If any of you would like a written transcript of that speech, all I can tell you is that you really ought to get out more often.

Well, as King Kong once said on top of the Empire State Building, 'Can't talk anymore, I've got to catch a plane.'

For the benefit of those gentlemen on Viagra, now's the time to swallow one; I'm coming to the end of the speech.

Well, that's about it. We've shared some laughs, we've shared some tears ... if anybody wants to share a cab, I'm open to offers ...

I've got to be going now ... I'm entered in a brandy-drinking contest and I want to see who comes in second!

If you've enjoyed listening to this speech as much as I've enjoyed making it, then all I can do is apologise most sincerely.

It's been a real pleasure to be here; I'd like to say thank you for having me – and to those of you who haven't, please be patient.

I leave you with this thought:
Always try to keep a smile on your face, because it'd look silly on your arse.

My horoscope this morning said, 'This is your lucky day. People will be so moved by your words and captivated by your charm and your wit, that they will rise to their feet at the end of your speech in a spontaneous standing ovation!' Ladies and gentlemen, I leave it to you – do you want to make a liar out of Mystic Meg?

EMCEE LINES
(Master of Ceremonies)

... and now a big surprise, so close your hands and hold out your eyes!

As you may have noticed, Lionel Morris was not due to make a speech this evening, but, I've been walking around and eliciting a few opinions, and it's now become a matter of popular demand ... Everyone I spoke to made a point of *insisting* ... that Lionel didn't make a speech tonight.

Tonight is indeed, a Gala night. And, believe me, it's a long time since I could manage a gal-a-night!
(Bridging line)

And now for a guy who took so much Viagra, he had to go to a shrink.

Our guest speaker this evening has a wealth of knowledge and experience. I'm pleased to tell you that tonight, he's ready to share with us everything he knows, so ... (look at watch) ... we should be out of here in about three minutes.

The next speaker is best described as a legend in his own time.
His own time is five minutes ... and he'd better not over-run!

Many of you, I'm sure, will have recognised our next speaker, but before you ask for your money back ...

I have to warn you, he is a bit long-winded ... in fact, he only sat down three days ago from *last* year's speech!

I don't know how long Sidney Stafford will be speaking this evening, I didn't help him write his speech ... but I think I ought to warn you, I *did* help him carry it in.

I hear that Sidney's speech is going to be quite serious ... there won't be any jokes.
Well of course, with a suit like that, who needs jokes?

Sidney has the reputation of being one of the best speakers in the country ... unfortunately, this is the city.

And now someone who was born with a silver foot in his mouth ...

I can introduce him, but I can't guarantee him.

Our next speaker is a man of great dignity, integrity, charisma and ... oh sorry, no it's not – it's Ian Parkin!

I now propose that we take a ten minute break ... those of you who fell asleep can wake up, and those of you who stayed awake can have a kip.

FUNERALS AND WAKES
(and why not?)

If you are ever called upon to deliver a eulogy, the tone of your speech should depend very much upon the age of the deceased and the circumstances of their death. Your function is to comfort close friends and family members without resorting to excruciating platitudes or clichés.

There is often a place in a eulogy for some gentle and respectful humour, particularly if the deceased happened to be a bit of a character. Relate one or two light-hearted anecdotes if you can, and close on an inspiring, positive message.

The following, although not exactly one-liners, may nevertheless be of some use at funerals and wakes. After all, let's be honest, you do have to be a little stiff to appreciate them.

We come into this world naked and bare,
We go through this world with sorrow and care,
We go out of this world, we know not where,
But if we're good fellows here, we'll be
thoroughbreds there.

AN IRISH TOAST: Let not the devil hear of his death till he's safe inside the walls of Heaven.

To be born a gentleman is an accident –
To die one is an accomplishment.

I can let you into a little secret. His will reads, 'Being of sound mind, I spent all my money.'

'Oh here's to other meetings,
And merry greetings then,
And here's to those we've drunk with,
But never can again.'

(Stephen Decatur)

Sympathy is thinking with your heart.

'I am ready to meet my maker. Whether my maker is prepared for the great ordeal of meeting me is another matter.'

(Sir Winston Churchill)

'He first deceased; she for a little tried
To live without him, liked it not, and died.'

(Sir Henry Wotton)

Here are some more lines connected with funerals and wakes. Don't use these on the day, unless you have a very cool crowd indeed:

He was always ahead of his time, at the forefront of everything. In fact, he talked his priest into giving him 'first rites'.

What an organiser he was. If he'd have been running this funeral, we'd have all been down the pub by now.

Epitaph: 'At last, he's caught up with his jokes.'

Epitaph: 'Poor God.'

I've decided to have my body preserved in a Cryogenic chamber ... I'm also going to have my assets frozen at the same time so I won't be skint when they thaw me out.

The whole family cried at Uncle Leo's cremation ... somebody remembered his will was in his back pocket!

We're now going to hear a few words from Sean, who today is a bit like our dear departed friend over there ... he's necessary for the party, but nobody expects him to say too much.

HECKLE LINES

I caused a bit of a scene once at a meeting, when I described a fellow director's pompous outburst as a 'Crie d'arse'.

To this day, I'm not really sure whether that made me the heckler or the hecklee. Either way, I thought I deserved a round of applause.

Night Club comics often have to cope with loudmouth drunks and various nasty customers. The comedian is usually well-armed with several lines designed to turn the tables on the smart-arse and to get an extra laugh or two at the heckler's expense.

As a general rule, however, most heckling is very good-natured and restrained. It would be rather heavy-handed, if not churlish, for a speaker like you to learn professional anti-heckler lines simply for the purpose of silencing someone who is simply enjoying the evening.

So here they are:

Listen, I don't mind you heckling me, but there are people here trying to get some sleep!

Hey, I like that suit ... where d'you get it shined?

If I gave a shit, you'd be the first person I'd give it to.

You know, you don't look bad in men's clothes, you really should wear 'em more often!

Would you mind turning round? I hate to laugh in your face!

I like your approach … now let's see your departure.

I'm getting *paid* to act like a prick … what's your excuse?

You know, you really shouldn't drink on an empty head.

(To a female heckler. If you're brave enough)

… is that a real groan, or are you faking orgasms again?

Isn't she a treasure? I wonder who dug her up.

Well, if it isn't Joanna Lumley … and it isn't.

Look! A bombed blondshell.

(Rowdy crowd)

> **Would you mind keeping it down in the cocaine section, please?**

> **Carry on like this and I won't get to the funny stuff!**

(After a result)

> **Why don't you quit while you're behind?**

(After a very long question)

> **Thank you, you've really added something to today's programme ... five minutes, forty seconds!**

ICE-BREAKERS

I must say I find Roseanne Barr rather difficult to love, but some of her lines are tremendous. How about this for a really great ice-breaker. At a recent personal appearance, she opened by asking:

> 'How many men here are impotent?'

Roseanne surveyed the crowd, waiting in vain for a reaction. Then she said:

> 'Oh, I see you can't get your arms up either.'

Here are some others:

> **Good evening, I'm your first speaker of the evening – I'm here to break the ice ... and we all know what happened to the Titanic, don't we?!**

> **Don't worry if you happen to fall asleep during my speech, it often happens. I take it as a compliment; it means you trust me.**

(Lowering microphone):
> **If I'd listened to my mother and stood up straight, I wouldn't have to do this.**

> **Firstly, have any of you heard me speak before?**
> *(Look around)*
> **Well, it's the same old crap again, I'm afraid.**

> **Hello, my name is Mitch and I'm an alcoholic ... oops, sorry, wrong meeting!**

> **Before I continue ladies and gentlemen, Marks and Spencer Plc have asked me to announce that the suit I'm wearing this evening ... is from ... C & A.**

> **Now, all those of you who believe in telekinesis, please raise my hand.**

> **What we intend to do today is make this a 'nuts and bolts' discussion ...**
> **My name is Jerry Farr ... I'm one of the nuts.**

I'm going to be your Master of Ceremonies this evening, and at this stage, frankly, there's bugger all you can do about that ... so why don't we all just try to relax and it'll be over before you know it. Right?

See also 'Openers'.

IN A MARQUEE

Welcome to the marquee ... de *Sade*!

It's always a source of amazement to me, when I see what they can do with marquees these days. I really admire the way a team of experts comes in, and – in a few hours – creates a beautiful setting out of a few simple materials.
So this evening I feel truly honoured to have been given the opportunity of proposing a toast in a room that used to be Vanessa Feltz's nightie!

My congratulations to Sarah on cooking such a lovely meal for us. You know, it's been quite a challenge for her – helping to organise the party, acting as hostess and feeding a hundred and forty hungry people under canvas with the aid of just one camp stove. What a girl!

MISCELLANEOUS TIME-WASTERS

I was sitting in my office the other day, looking out over the Hudson River ... which is rather weird because my office is in Kilburn ...

A grasshopper walks into a bar and orders a beer. The barman says, 'You know, we have a drink named after you.' The grasshopper says, 'Blimey! You've got a drink called Kevin?!'

Somewhere along the line, Pete was introduced to Hazel and was immediately smitten. In fact, he'd never been so smut.

Two men walked into a bar ... you'd have thought *one* of them would have seen it.

He used to date this Native American girl, but every time he took her dancing, it started to rain.

She ran away from home, but several days later they found her safe ... they never did find *her*, but at least the safe was fine.

What a battle! Three brave men against a thousand ...
Boy! did we beat the shit out of those three!

(from Cindy Peroux)

When the doctor announced: 'It's a boy!', his father took one look at the kid and asked for a second opinion!

Tonight's movie stars Nadia Legova in the tragic story of a doomed woman who finally cast aside this mortal coil ... and went back on the pill!

NERVES

Use these lines if your nerves are a hot topic and you feel like being self-deprecating. Be aware, however, that it's rarely a wise policy to remind the audience how nervous you are.

I must admit, I was a little nervous earlier on, but I'm really at my ease now because I've realised I'm in front of my own kind of people ... piss artists!

I was so worried about this speech, I haven't slept for days and days! ... It's a bloody good thing I've been sleeping at night!

I haven't been this nervous since my holiday flight last year when the navigator stopped me in the aisle and asked me the way to the toilet!

I always wondered ... if God had a nervous breakdown, would he see people?

I've been so anxious about having to make this speech, that I even asked the wine waiter to recommend something that goes well with fingernails.

OPENERS

Ladies and gentlemen, in conclusion I'd like to ... oh sorry, wrong page.
(Place top page at the bottom of the script and start speech.)
Good evening everyone ...

Ooh, I feel so good today, I can hardly wait to hear what I have to say!

This won't be a long speech; I don't have that large a vocabulary.

There are some things that, in the interests of good taste, are better left unsaid. Well ... I'm here to say them!

(After opening applause)
How come I never get that sort of applause at the *end* of my speeches?

For those of you who don't know me, I've been involved with the newspaper industry for the last sixteen years ... For those of you who *do* know me, that's a load of bullshit.

Let me first of all assure you that I won't be keeping you long.
I've decided to speak fast because my material's lousy.

You know, I've always believed that if you can't laugh at yourself, at least take the piss out of somebody else ...
and it's in this spirit that I address you all this evening.

(When you've spoken to the same group before)
I must say, I count myself lucky to have been asked back to speak to you all for a second time ... most people only get to die once.

(When you're the last speaker after a long programme)
It's always good to get a chance to speak before they start putting the chairs on the tables.

As some of you may know, I'm here for two main reasons. Firstly, the organisers wanted to find a well-informed, entertaining personality with expertise ... and they did.
The second reason is, he got the flu so they phoned *me*.

You know, participating in a conference of this calibre means a lot more to me than merely the strengthening of international ties, it means more than just prestige, more than acceptance by my peers ... it means ... a bloody great piss-up!

See also 'Ice-Breakers'.

PHILOSOPHY

There's nothing like a big broad smile ... but then of course, there's nothing like a big broad!

There are two times in life when you are totally and utterly alone: just before you die, and just before you make a speech.

Time is what keeps everything from happening at once.

What if there were no hypothetical questions?

If great minds think alike, what do great arses do?

No use being pessimistic – it wouldn't work anyway.

He who ties string around fingers, usually remembers to buy yo-yo.

Men are from Mars, Women are from Venus ... where the hell did Julian Clary come from?

'Progress might have been all right once, but it's gone on entirely too long.'

(Ogden Nash)

REPLY LINES

Thank you for those words ... I'm really impressed; I never realised you could buy jokes at Woolworths!

I'd like to compliment you on a great speech ... so please, as soon as you make one, let me know, won't you?!

As I was listening to those glowing remarks, I have to admit that my primary thought was about what they were full of.

FOLLOWING FLATTERING BUILD-UP:

I only wish I had the time to disagree with you, but I'm a busy man.

A few more introductions like that and I can stop going for therapy.

Well, that was quite an introduction. Obviously, nobody believed it, otherwise they wouldn't be sitting, they'd be kneeling. But thank you anyway.

ROASTS, INSULTS AND CHARACTER ASSASSINATIONS

I must say it's quite an experience, standing up here tonight, surrounded by 'la crème de la scum' ...

I feel honoured to have been asked to pay tribute to a really talented man, admired and loved by everyone ...
Unfortunately, he couldn't make it, so I'm stuck with the job of taking the piss out of *this* poor sod!

This is a man who loves pasta better than sex ... of course, that's probably because he can *get* pasta.

It's impossible to praise this guy too highly ...
In fact it's impossible to praise him at all ... he's crap!

This man has the most wonderful and remarkable parents; parents who possess a very rare kind of brilliance ... the kind of brilliance that skips a generation.

Over eighty million sperm and his had to be the one that made it!

He has two basic problems: he thinks everybody else is better ... and everybody else does too.

He hasn't an enemy in the world, he doesn't need 'em ... all his friends hate him.

He's an ordinary sort of a guy; forty-two around the chest, thirty-six around the waist, ninety-five around the golf course ... and a pain in the arse around the house.

'How infuriating is he?' I hear you ask. Well I'll tell you how infuriating: two years ago, Salman Rushdie put a fatwah out on *him*!

He's a sex symbol for women who just don't care anymore.

His ambition is to be filthy rich ... well, so far, he's halfway there.

Don't worry, I'm not going to make fun of Pete Martin; I can't stand people who make fun of someone just because they're bloody useless!

Actually, this man is outstanding. In fact, that's where I met him ...
he was out standing in front of the Job Centre.

(Bridging line)

All sorts of things happen to this guy; last week, a girl stopped him in the street and said, 'Hello, you gorgeous handsome hunk ... could you show me the way to Specsavers?'

But you see, I admire talented people ...
On the other hand, I like Robin Morgan as well.

To me, Robin is like the brother I never had, so now at least I know for sure that if I'd *had* a brother ... he would have been a pain in the arse.

Robin was a premature baby ... he was born three months before his parents had a chance to get married.

He was named in this year's Honours list ... it read: 'He's not getting one'.

Nevertheless, in this industry, Robin is regarded as Nobility! ... He has no 'bility at all!

SAVERS AND AD LIBS

These lines are designed to make you look wittier than you really are so I suggest you keep a few of the best ones hanging from your belt. When an appropriate situation arises, grab one, remove the pin with your teeth, and lob it into the audience.

Be a psychic; anticipate the reaction to something you've said, and have the follow-up ready. That way, if your first gag is weakly received, it'll look like a deliberate 'plant' rather than something that didn't quite work.

Stick with me kid and I'll show you how to be a big bad son-of-a-bitch like me!

AFTER A SLIP-UP:

If you think *that* was a mistake, you should have seen my first wife!

That's the first time this ever happened again.

NO LAUGHS:

Come on! I know you're out there – I can hear you yawning!

Well you had to be there ... and I wish I were there right now!

What are you, an audience or a jury?

(To someone at the door)
Start the car!

A memorial service for that joke will be held at 2 p.m. this coming Sunday.

You know, I wish I had a hundred gags like that one ... unfortunately, I've got a thousand!

(Tap mike)
Is this thing on?

Don't blame me, I stole these jokes from Jack Dee.

That was my DHL joke ... you should get it within twenty-four hours.

I don't have to be here at all, you know; I could have phoned the speech in!

Well, who'd have thought the end of the world would have come on a Friday?

I must say you're taking this awfully well.

I'll give you five seconds more on that one.

Oh well, back to the jokes!

QUIPS:

As you see, I work from notes ... I make the same number of mistakes, but at least I have them documented!

(Someone leaves during your speech)

Don't tell me, let me guess ... you're so impressed by my speech you're going out to tell your friends, right?

Okay, okay ... a little boredom never hurt anyone!

One thing's for certain ... nobody knows for sure.

BIG LAUGHS (What a lovely problem) :

Save it please, I've got a lousy finish.

(Hand up)

Please, this is a very old building!

(Following big or extended laughter from one person)

Do you mind? ... Somebody's got to sit in that chair after you!

HOT ROOM:

I'd like to take a quick poll ... All those of you who are sweating from this heat, please *don't* raise your hands.

COLD ROOM:

Ladies and gentlemen, I'd like to announce that today's proceedings are being sponsored by Zanussi Refrigeration.

WATER SET-UP LINES:

Excuse me while I take a sip of my Smirnoff mineral water.

Looks just like water, doesn't it?

POOR ATTENDANCE:

This must be a very wealthy club, I see each one of you bought two seats!

Did you all come in the same car?

As you can see, we have a very small turnout this evening and you can probably blame that on the publicity ... too many people knew I was going to be speaking tonight.

Thank you ... you're a great bunch of seats!

SILLY STUFF

Watch out for the brand new movie: 'The Paper Towel That Soaked Up Blackburn.'

Jesus is coming ... look busy!

'To be is to do' – Jean-Paul Sartre, 'To do is to be' – Solzhenitsyn, 'Doo be doo be doo' – Frank Sinatra.

I'll never forget my grandfather's last words ... 'Shit! A truck!'

Very funny Scotty ... now beam down my clothes!

The Rhythm Method is sex between two consenting adults ... and the Jools Holland Trio.

SMART-ARSE QUIPS

The first thing I'd like to say this evening is ... unfortunately I left all my credit cards at home so ... anybody got any cash?

I hope you don't mind if we take a break every fifteen minutes ... I'm double parked.

You know I can tell you've all had too much to drink ... every time you try to clap, you miss!

Gentlemen, I need your vote, your support, your trust ... and a jacket potato on the side.

Interesting room this; NASA used to train astronauts here, you know ... no atmosphere.

... but to be serious for a moment – and I might as well 'cos I'm not getting any laughs ...

... and if you're not confused by now, you're obviously not paying attention.

(After a statistic, a piece of trivia or an interesting fact)
... Ask yourselves, could you have got through the rest of the evening without knowing that?

I hate to spread rumours, but be fair, what else can you do with them?

TOASTS

We only propose toasts to see how many people are still capable of standing.

I drink to your health when I'm with you
I drink to your health when alone
I drink to your health so often
I've just about buggered my own!

Please join me in a toast to the Hay Fever Club ...
Here's looking at-choo!

Here's to you, here's to me
May we never disagree.
But if we do, to hell with you
And here's to me!

(After Loyal Toast)
... Ladies and gentlemen, you may now smoke.
Tobacco only please, you never know who's
sitting next to you.

Please join me now in a toast to the pleasure of
drinking:

There are several reasons for drinking,
And one has just entered my head
If a man cannot drink when he's living,
How the hell can he drink when he's dead?

TOASTS OF ALL NATIONS:

Arabic:	'Besalamati!' (Peace), 'Bismillah', 'Fi schettak'.
Belgian:	'Op Uw Gezonheid!' (To your health)
Chinese:	'Kan bei!', 'Wen lie', 'Nien Nien nu e'.
Danish:	'Skal'
Dutch:	'Proost!'
Finnish:	'Kippis'
French:	'A votre santé!' (To your health)
German:	'Prosit!'
Greek:	'Iss Igian!'
Irish Gaelic:	'Slainte!' (To your health)
Hindi:	'Aanand', 'Jaikind'
Hebrew:	'L' Chayim' (To life)
Italian:	'Cin cin', 'Salute'
Japanese:	'Kampai!', 'Banzai!'
Maori:	'Kia-Ora'

Norwegian: 'Skal'
Polish: 'Na zdrowie!' (To your health)
Portuguese: 'A sua saúde!' (Singular), 'Saude!' (To a group)
Russian: 'Na zdorovia'
Spanish: 'Salud' (Health)
Swedish: 'Skal'
Urdu: 'Sanda Bashi'
Welsh: 'Icchyd da'
Zulu: 'Oogy wawa!'

Check out pronunciation before using in your speech.

TRIBUTES

Dotted among the following lines are some examples of positive humour. Positive material is useful when you have to be amusing about someone without risking any disapproval. A patriarch, a distant boss, someone you don't know very well or any woman. By choosing lines where the subject comes out as a 'winner', you can be both funny and safe.
Yes – you creeping, crawling cringers – these lines are for you.

He has an incredibly strong and forceful personality. This is the guy to whom Frank Sinatra once said, 'All right then, we'll do it *your* way!'

This guy is a brilliant businessman. The best! To give you some idea, he was mugged by a street gang in Mayfair last week, and he made three hundred quid on the deal!

You know, sometimes there's a fine line between being 'given the honour' and being 'lumbered'. Well, tonight ladies and gentlemen, I'm honoured to have been lumbered with the task of paying tribute to ...

So tonight we honour a humble man ... a man who only ever wanted two things from this world: one – for his body to be sent to Guy's Hospital Research Unit when he passes on, and two – for it to be sent to The Spice Girls while he's still here.

Today, we honour Bob Prentice ... or, as he's known in scores of hotel registration forms ... John Smith.

You see? She's always smiling, always interested, always gracious ... always adhering to one sustaining thought ...
you can read it on her face tonight ...
'Who needs *this* shit?!'

He's got a stiff upper lip ... he's had it since he accidentally bit on a Viagra capsule.

I used to admire that stiff upper lip ... until I saw him trying to drink a glass of red wine. What a mess!

A lot of people are surprised that Bob is a friend of Cabinet Ministers, top entertainers, royalty ... but why not? Even *they* need someone to look up to.

For twenty-five years, he's been trapped in a good marriage.

He was always a bon viveur ... in fact, he was a gourmet toddler! When he sucked his thumb, he used to insist on dipping it in a béchamel sauce with parmesan.

This man is such a wonderful, saintly, honest person that when he goes to church, the priest confesses to *him*!

He's a corporate strategist, a consultant, an accountant, a raconteur, an athlete, a writer ... and on the seventh day, he rested ...

This man could charm the knickers off a transvestite!

Index